Etta's Song

Etta's Song

A BEAUTIFUL LIFE, A TRAGIC LOVE,
A STORY THAT MUST BE TOLD

DOMANIQUE WILLIAMS

Etta's Safe Haven
PUBLISHING

ETTA'S SONG
A Beautiful Life, a Tragic Love, a Story That Must Be Told

Paperback ISBN: 979-8-9911446-0-5

First Paperback Edition: December 2025

Edited by: Unpolished Words
Cover by: Make Your Mark Publishing Solutions
Layout by: Make Your Mark Publishing Solutions

"Through pain, I found my strength; Through love, I discovered my purpose."

~Domanique Williams

For my loving mother, between your strength, your laughter, and your memory, I have found my peace.

&

For my daughter, whose heart and courage gives me reason to continue honoring the legacy of love and resilience left behind.

Dear Reader,

Thank you for choosing this book. By doing so, you've taken an important step in understanding and raising awareness on domestic abuse in romantic relationships. As you delve into these pages, you may encounter difficult emotions and challenging content. My aim is not to sensationalize, but to shed light on the realities many face behind closed doors. This book explores the complexities of abusive relationships, the impact on survivors, and paths toward healing and prevention.

The support of reading and sharing your support helps break the silence surrounding domestic abuse. Together, we can foster open conversations, challenge harmful norms, and create safer communities. I'm deeply grateful for your willingness to engage upon this crucial issue. Whether you are a survivor, friend, family member, or someone seeking to understand, your awareness makes a difference.

Remember, help is always available. If you or someone you know is experiencing abuse, please reach out to local support services or national hotlines. Thank you for being a part of this important dialogue. Your support means much more than you know.

Lastly, as you enter into Etta's world and learn who she was, I ask that you continue to let her light shine. She shined with passion, love, and joy. She was so much more than just a mother and caretaker; she was a saving grace. Her story is not all roses and butterflies but it's her story. It's what made her who she was. She was a strong woman. A hopeful woman. A woman of unconditional love.

She has helped shape my life, as well as many others. With every memory I carry her, in every lesson I learn from her, and with her story I am her.

Although she is no longer with us in the flesh, her hands are no longer around to hold, her hugs are no longer around to embrace, and her voice is no longer physically heard, make no mistake that her spirit is with us and runs through every chapter of this book. I hope as you read these words you carry her with you too. Not because she was perfect but because she was human, she was real, and her story must be told.

With love and remembrance,
Domanique Williams

Dear Mama,

Words will never be enough to express how much you mean to me. There is not a day that goes by I don't think of you and how much I appreciate all you have done, even in your absence. It has been an honor to have you as my mother and best friend. I have no idea what my life would have been if I didn't have you to lean on or help guide me in times of need. You were always there when I needed you most and even when I was not aware that I needed you, you were there every step of the way to support me.

I have always been proud of the woman you were and proud to call you my mother. I am beyond grateful that God chose you to nurture, protect, and care for me. You put so much energy, time, kindness, and love into everything and everyone you have touched, near or far. Now it is my time to return that for you. I pray that I will be even half the woman you were in this lifetime. As I write this book to tell your story the best I know how, I pray that I have made you proud, that these words help others, and that you continue to live on through the men and women you have touched and inspired in such a way that they chose to learn, grow, speak out, and heal from your true story.

I Love You,
Baby Girl!

Contents

Introduction

This book was created from both pain and love, from the ache of losing my mother and the fire to tell her story with truth and dignity. Etta was a woman who faced more than her share of hardships, but through it all, she carried herself with grace, courage, and unshakable faith. Her life was taken by the hands of domestic violence, but in these pages, her story deserved to be told. Not as a tragedy but as a testimony of endurance, faith, and love.

Writing this memoir was not easy. It meant revisiting wounds I once tried to forget, but also discovering the healing that comes from speaking her name out loud. I wanted to give her story the light it deserved. To turn pain into purpose and silence into strength. This book is my way of saying that her life mattered, her voice mattered, and her love still echoes through every chapter.

To my daughter—you are my why. Your light gave me the courage to finish what pain tried to silence. You inspire me every day to stand stronger, to love harder, and to heal openly. May you always carry your grandmother's strength within you and remember that you come from a line of powerful women who refused to be defined by what tried to break them.

This book is for both of you—one who gave me life, and one who gives me reason to live it fully.

My hope is that these words remind you all to never give up

on healing, growth, or love, even when the road is uncertain. This story comes from real experiences, moments of love, loss, confusion, and clarity. I share it not for sympathy, but for connection. Healing is not linear, and we all carry stories that deserve to be heard.

If even one reader finds comfort, understanding, or hope within these pages, then my purpose has been fulfilled. Thank you for allowing me to share our story with you.

Mama's mom
(Grandma Johnnie
Mae Williams)

Mama's dad
(Grandad Robert Williams
AKA Ballgame)

Chapter 1

Introducing Etta

J ohnnie "Etta" Williams was born in the small town of Swainsboro, Georgia, on September 21, 1970, to Robert (aka "Ballgame") and Johnnie Mae Williams, along with one sister and five brothers. She is the sixth child. She was called by her middle name as a young girl because she and her mother shared the same first name. She was a loving, peaceful, and happy child with a very close relationship with her parents and siblings growing up.

In her teen years, she began dating and, at the age of fifteen, found out that she was pregnant. But early in her second trimester she developed complications that led to her having a miscarriage. It was a baby boy. Etta continued school while grieving her relationship and the loss of her baby boy, but she began to lose her motivation to continue. She dropped out.

When Etta was sixteen, she was introduced to a man name Thurston, known as "Bug," by her older sister. They were friends in school together and Grandma Johnnie was fond of him. She encouraged the relationship between Etta and Bug, because he showed to be a promising young man, and shortly after meeting, they began dating. After about two years of dating, Bug moved in with her at her mother's home. She became pregnant with another baby boy when she was eighteen, and they named him Sterlyng. They were excited.

Grandma Johnnie was protective of Etta's pregnancy. She made sure Etta was safe and taking things easy around the house. She told her it was best to stay in the house and rest, and that she couldn't even go out to check the mailbox, because she needed to stay off her feet. She told Bug that he had no choice but to take care of her baby girl, and he did. He stayed by her side and continued working as a truck driver, which he had been doing since the age of seventeen. Bug took care of Etta. She had everything she needed, and she stayed home to take care of her baby boy as a stay-at-home mom. Sterlyng was born in December of 1988 with a heart murmur. This devastated Etta, because she was not sure how to deal with this at such a young age herself. Three months later, she found out that they had conceived again: a baby girl they named Kaisha. Kaisha was also born with a heart murmur in December of 1989, when Etta was nineteen. She and Bug decided that they would have no more children, because two was enough and it was a lot to deal with. Then, they moved from Etta's mother's house to Bug's father's home in Cross and Green.

While living with Bug's father, Etta continued to raise her children as a stay-at-home mom for a while, until she started doing house cleaning for Bug's boss and his family.

Dad standing in the yard with Sterlyng and Kaisha enjoying family

Etta wanted to be married. As a little girl, she dreamed of being married and having a family, like most of us do. She wondered why Bug hadn't asked her yet. When she finally summoned the courage to have a conversation with him about getting married, he explained to her that he just wasn't ready yet. She continued house cleaning and taking care of the children until she was twenty-one, when she became pregnant again. It was a shock because they had already decided they were done. Although they didn't want another kid, they decided together to take on the responsibility and had another baby girl. Domanique (that's me) was born in March of 1992. Dad calls me Boo-Boo. Now Etta and Bug have three children, all born with heart murmurs.

It was a lot to take on, and they had a long road ahead, but they did it together. Etta and Bug were serious about not having any more children this time. They worried that if they did, they would also be born with heart murmurs, so she decided to have her tubes tied.

Etta's sister gave each of her children their first names. Naming us was the last thing on Etta's mind, since she was concerned about each of us having heart murmurs. Taking us back and forth to a heart specialist in Augusta, Georgia, was a lot on her, especially while Dad was on the road. As kids, my sister's and my heart murmurs began to close slowly, and eventually, they closed completely.

Before I turned three, Grandad became ill and passed away, so Dad would return home from driving as often as he could to help. Sterlyng's heart murmur seemed like it was closing little by little, but it wasn't completely closing. Etta worried herself and became more protective of him and everything he did. She watched his every move.

Again, in the midst of everything going on with her children, Etta made it known that she wanted to be married. Dad still felt that he wasn't ready. He was OK with the way things were with his family; it all seemed fine as it was, to him.

Dad set the tone for how a woman should be treated with care. We experienced and witnessed true and gentle love, even when there were flaws, which they kept private and separate from us. He spoke to and handled Mom with love and was gentle to her. He didn't disrespect her with his words, never harmed her in any way, gave her everything she needed, and was a provider. His way of showing his love to her was through the way he took care of her, making sure she had everything and was happy. It was all he wanted to do, his priority. He experienced some abuse in his parents' relationship when he was younger and, after seeing what his father had done to his mother, made the decision that he was going to be a better man. And he is. He believes there are many ways to express yourself without being physically or emotionally harmful.

This played a huge part in how we were disciplined by him. Dad is a more laid back and chill type of guy. He treated us the same, with love and gentleness. And he's against physical discipline when it comes to children, or anyone for that matter. When we were kids, he wouldn't allow anyone to whoop us in his presence, and if anyone tried, he would stop it from happening. Once, he popped Kaisha because she was acting up and crying while we were at a family member's house. It hurt his feelings so badly that he cried, and never did it again. However, Mama wasn't against it. She set the rules and disciplined us as she saw fit.

Dad has always been my safe space. My favorite place to sleep and my comfort zone; where I always felt safe as a little girl was on my daddy's belly, where I slept. He's always had a round belly, and any chance I could, I would fall asleep on him—but not before he would bring out the huge black bible that sat on his dresser. We would gather around and lie across their bed or the floor, and Dad would read and teach us about God. Sometimes it sounded like he was preaching to us, then he would pray and send us to bed. I would cry all night at their bedroom door until Mama let me in while Dad was snoring. He snored loud enough to hear it through the walls, but it never kept me from sleeping on his belly. I was safe.

They took us on many family trips every summer to Daytona, Florida, to see family members and enjoy the beach. Etta was a passenger princess, so Dad did the driving while she sat, smiled, and sight saw as he drove to different cities and states. I sat between them while everyone else was sleeping and talked Dad's ear off with every trip. But as soon as we got to our destination, I would fall asleep instantly. He would also bring us in the big truck sometimes, so we could travel with him. We were not allowed to visit certain places, so Mama would hide with us in the back where the bed was, close the curtains, and tell us to be quiet. It was a quiet game we played, and we loved it, softly giggling and whispering to each other. Or sometimes, Dad would drop us off at a nearby store for more snacks and drinks while he made his drops and pickups.

Although life may have been great through the eyes of their children, Mama and Dad's relationship was marred with dishonesty and ended when I was five years old. It's funny how memory works, how we can remember such things as a young child. It was not fairy tales and butterflies every day, as we thought we knew it to be. We were young but sad that our family was separating. It felt like the worst thing was happening to us.

Near the end, I walked to the doorway of Mom and Dad's bedroom as they were speaking back and forth. I could sense something was wrong by their voices, facial expressions, and body language. Mama's face looked upset, and Dad's looked disappointed, and his voice wasn't so soft. They were both standing at their headboard while Mom packed her clothes into a bag on the bed. Dad continued to talk to her and ask her if she was sure that she wanted to go, and she demanded that he let her leave. He touched her arm, but she pulled back. She grabbed her bag and walked toward the door. I felt sad.

Kaisha began to cry in the other room, and Sterlyng decided to run through the front door and run away. He ran out of the house but didn't go far. We searched for him at the neighbor's and around the house. After an hour or so of looking for him and yelling his name, we found him in one of Mama's old cars that was still sitting at the back of the house. He never actually ran away, but to him, he did, and he thought this would stop our family from breaking up. It didn't.

We lived with Dad for a while, and family members helped take on the load of looking after us, because Dad was still driving trucks. They made sure we ate and went to school and church. Dad's niece even moved in with us for a while to make sure someone kept their eyes on us so Dad wouldn't have to worry.

Etta was a loving and caring woman, a devoted mother who loved God and had the purest heart you would have ever known. She loved everyone, literally, and would tell you so every chance she spoke with you, no matter who you were. Even a stranger would receive her love and kindness in her presence. But she had things to figure out; she was only human.

Mama standing outside in her sister's yard

Chapter 2

New Beginnings

E tta moved into an apartment on Racetrack Street. She made the apartment a place for us to live together again, but without Dad. This was new to us, because we had always been a family under one roof. Sterlyng mainly wanted to stay with Dad, so he was not with us a lot of the time. Kaisha and I moved with Mama, though, and then shortly after, Grandad moved in after becoming ill.

While caring for Ballgame, Mama began dating. We were not aware of exactly who he was at first, because she didn't introduce us to him in the beginning. All we knew was his name, Henry, and that he was a tall dark-skinned guy.

Grandad was tall too. He was a tall brown-skinned handsome fella. I don't remember much of Grandad, but I do know how much he loved us and remember how he would lie on the couch in his favorite spot. He always had a little "piece of change," as he would say, or peppermint to give all his grandchildren whenever we were around. Grandad didn't talk much because he was not in the best physical position then, but he was as present in our lives as he could be, and for that we will always remember him. He lived with us for a brief time, until his very last moments. He passed away in July of 1997.

After his passing, Mama found it in her heart to start caring for others as she did her father. She began classes to become a Certified Nursing Assistant (CNA). Etta graduated September of 1999, then became an employee at PruittHealth, a nursing home of Swainsboro in November of 1999.

As she and Henry continued seeing each other, she decided to introduce him to us as her "friend." He smiled with shining gold teeth in his mouth. He told us his name and became a friend of ours as well. We would laugh and play together all the time, and our favorite thing to do was watch wrestling at night. Mama would say it was bedtime, but he insisted we all stay up late and watch it. I liked staying up late watching wrestling.

Henry became a mean man, but he said he loved us, and Mama. Nothing we started to see in Henry was what Dad showed us a man should be. As a seven-year-old girl, I may not have understood everything, but I knew that this kind of "love" was hurtful. It made Mama sad all the time, and I didn't like it. This was different. It was a silenced and painful kind of love. It left her black and blue, depressed, crying, fearful, and struggling. We were confused and scared, and we didn't know who to talk to about what was happening.

He was mad at Mama all the time, especially if things weren't the way he liked or expected. He would yell and break things, like the kitchen window. And Mama would have to call the head office and lie and tell them that her kids were throwing a ball around and accidentally broke it so that we wouldn't get kicked out. He punched, kicked, slapped, and beat her for what seemed like no reason at all. We would sit there and cry as we watched the beatings and yelling, every single time. We'd even sneak and tell Dad.

Dad often let Etta know that no matter what, he was still there for her, and if she ever needed to "come home," she could. He assured her of this and meant every word. He still loved her. She was the first woman he had ever loved. When he told her that it was OK to come home, he meant that if she ever needed him and wanted to come back home with him, or wanted to get away, that she could. He would do whatever he could to protect her.

Henry controlled Etta's being, what she wore, where she could and couldn't go, who she could and couldn't talk to, and even what she looked at while driving. When Mama took us places, she had to drive looking straight ahead. And if it seemed she looked at someone on the side of the road or anything, he became angry with her, calling her names and saying hurtful things to her while we sat in the back seat. She was terrified of him and wanted to get away but ended back with him every time.

When we moved from the apartment and into a duplex home, we noticed he was in the streets a lot, but we didn't understand exactly why at the time. Once, she decided to switch the bedrooms around while he was out to give us more space, because it was only two bedrooms, and we needed the bigger room for the three of us. When he came home, he saw what she had done and was furious. He abused her while we cried in our room, listening to each hit, each word he yelled at her, demanding that she change it back. She didn't, and the next thing I knew, police were knocking down our door looking for him.

We were actually happy that he was taken away, because that meant Mama would finally be free from him, and we would be too.

While he was locked away, he would call every chance he could to make sure she was working on getting him out, and she was. Mama was scared and made sure she did exactly as he demanded to make him happy, but he still abused her, and she began to lose everything.

Etta lost her duplex and the van she drove at the time. We moved in with her aunt and sometimes stayed with other family members until he got out, when we moved into a hotel. We stayed there for a while. We could have moved in with Dad, but we wanted to be with Mama and to make sure she was OK. We caught a taxi to school every day, and Mama still made sure we had hot meals there until we were kicked out. Henry was upset about something and tackled Mama into the wall. There she laid, in a hole in the wall, while we screamed and cried out for help. Her eyes were closed and her body was limp. We felt powerless and small because it seemed we couldn't do anything to help her. The owner had had enough of the disturbances Henry caused.

Eventually, Mama was approved to rent another apartment on Racetrack Street, where she decided enough was enough. One day, they were arguing as usual. Sterlyng was with us at the time, and he was tired of the abuse, so he spoke up for Mama. Henry wasn't pleased and began arguing with him too. Honestly, the three of us were tired of all this and voiced our opinions. It frightened Etta, because she knew what Henry was capable of once he was angry. She could deal with him being angry with her, but her children were off limits. After eight years of the relationship, that was the last straw.

When he left for a few hours, she asked us to quickly help her put all his belongings into big black trash bags and place them onto the porch. We did. It was the happiest feeling I had felt. I was proud of her. She was nervous and worried about what his actions would be once he returned to his things outside, but she had to choose her children now.

When he returned, the screen and front door were both locked. He knocked on the door and shouted for Mama to let him in, but she said no, and to go away. But he didn't. He continued to knock and ask for one of us to unlock the doors. He called out to me in a sweet voice to let him in, but Mama told me not to open the door. I went to the front door and unlocked it, looked at him, and faked like I was going to unlock the screen door, but I didn't. Instead, I mocked him and said, "Ha ha, you can't come in," before laughing and closing and locking the door.

We never saw him again. It took a while for Mama to see herself in the mirror as she once did. She continued to work, take care of her children, and keep her spirit up. Mama lost herself in those years, but her return was beautiful.

As a mother, Etta was always there, even when we were in the wrong, to lecture and encourage us. We didn't always behave as we should as children. We fought others and each other, got suspended from school, talked back sometimes, and had attitudes as teens do. When Sterlyng decided to leave school, she still encouraged him. When I would "run away" and ride the bus to my dad's house without anyone's knowledge, she still loved me. Mama smiled, gave us hugs and gentle touches, and always said, "I love you." She didn't skip a single day. Even if she didn't have it in her or had nothing left to give, she did it and gave anyway.

No matter what challenges Mama was facing, we wanted to be by her side. The way she loved us was more than I could have ever asked for. We weren't perfect, but we were hers, and she loved us.

Etta was five feet, four inches. She had brown skin with a few meaningful tattoos, black hair, brown eyes with the left eye slightly drooped, and a thin gap between her two front teeth. She always smelled good, even if she couldn't pronounce the fragrance. She took pride in the way she looked and smelled and kept her hair done. She had this unforgettable, contagious laugh, and she ate ice so annoyingly but also in a funny way, because of how her mouth would form while chewing. She had the strongest and finest legs and arms, which we believed came from her job's duties.

She shared many stories with us of how she helped lift, feed, and bathe residents if they required help. She shared the good and sometimes the bad of her work but never once complained. She would even use her own money to purchase the residents' favorite snacks, body wash and perfumes, socks, hats, blankets, and whatever else they seemed to need or want. She did this because she cared.

If a resident fell ill, Etta sat with them at the hospital after work, patiently watching over them for hours at a time, even though they were in good hands, because to her, they were still *her* residents. She was not leaving them alone. She worried herself. On days she was off and not watching *The Young and the Restless*, she sat and ate with them just to talk and make sure they were OK, or she called to check in. They were always a part of her. She grew attached to each one of her residents, and with that, she grew many relationships with their families as well. She became well known for her care and love for others. There were also friends and family members placed at the nursing home that she looked after as well.

Nursing and caring for others were Etta's true callings. She took pride in her job and what she was doing for others. It was a challenge convincing her to take vacations to relax and enjoy herself. We felt She pushed herself too much, but it was not just a job to her; it was her life and part of what made her the woman she was. It was her passion.

My great grandmother Martha Woods AKA "Grandma Doll"

Chapter 3

Grief and Blessings Entwined

Johnnie Mae was the queen of the family. She was one of eleven children her mother birthed. Johnnie Mae helped take care of her mother, Martha Woods (aka "Grandma Doll"), along with others, until she passed away in 2003. Grandma was very blunt and honest; she said what was on her mind and kept everyone in check, no matter who you were or your age. Mama took us to Grandma's house in the country on weekends to sit with her. She had plenty of stuffed bears in the far bedroom of her trailer, little glass fixtures everywhere, and other things around the house that we wanted to get our hands on, but Grandma didn't allow us to touch them. She was strict about her things.

She had plants in the kitchen that grew very long. They wrapped around the kitchen, following along the ceiling, and I would gaze at them every visit to see how much more they had grown. I was fascinated by how long they were becoming.

Grandma and Mama would talk while food cooked. When it was done, Grandma would have us place newspaper onto the floor for us to sit on and eat the food she had prepared for us. Then, Mama would pull out a kitchen chair to do Grandma's hair. Mama would gently scratch Grandma's scalp with a little black comb before she washed it. Grandma's hair was very fine and curly. She loved her curls. After blow drying her hair, Mama then greased her scalp very lightly with Blue Magic hair conditioner as we watched and finished our food. Then we were sent outside to play as they talked because children had no business listening to "grown folk" talk.

Some days Grandma would have peas for us to snap, which felt like it took forever to do, but we did it anyway, sitting on newspaper or a bucket. We played around with RJ, Grandma's parrot. He would repeat "RJ pretty bird," because that's what she called him, and he learned to mock it. Outside, there was a big tree in the yard with a bench below, where we sat in the shade. The neighbors to the right side of the house had cows that we would see. Grandma had dogs, bunnies, roosters, and chickens. Sometimes she had us go out to the chicken coop and collect the eggs for her, and we got to take them home when we left. We were chased a few times but never bitten.

Grandma made certain foods that I had never eaten or liked, such as okra and squash. I hated okra, especially if it wasn't fried, because I didn't like the texture, but I ate it anyway because if she cooked it, you had no choice but to eat. I also tried coffee for the first time with her, and I loved the way she made it. I loved the smell of coffee and how sweet she made it for me, with just the right amount of creamer to make the color the same as my brown skin. She would make it for me when we visited. Grandma was a very short, sweet, and sassy little lady, and we all loved her, but she fell sick suddenly when she was 59 years old. We said our goodbyes in June of 2006.

Etta was a mama's girl. After losing her mother, she changed. We watched her smile dim with each visit to the hospital to see Grandma. At first, she wouldn't bring us to the hospital, but when things didn't seem to change and Grandma's organs began to fail, Etta decided that it was time. I remember walking into the room to see grandma. I was fourteen years old and nervous, because I wasn't sure that I wanted to see her yet. This was the first time in my life that I had experienced something like this—sickness and grief—because I was only two and five years old when my grandfathers passed away, not quite understanding what death was. I couldn't express what I was feeling, but I knew that I was sad as I walked into her room. There were tubes hooked to her as I stood at her bedside.

Etta became depressed and took a break from college. She had just started taking nursing classes to become a Registered Nurse (RN) right before her mother's passing. She lay in her dark room and cried herself to sleep many days and nights as we sat by the door listening and waiting. We waited for her to pick herself back up, to smile again, and to continue with her degree, but she never went back to school. She lost her motivation to become a registered nurse and went back to work as a CNA, where she received certifications for hard work and dedication. She received a certificate for completing the National Council of Certified Dementia Practitioners, and more.

Even through grief and everything Mama was silently dealing with, she was still our biggest supporter. In September of 2008, Etta had something to smile for again. It eased some of her pain and kept her going: She became a grandmother. Although it was quite a bit of a shock, she was excited because, to her, her first grandchild was her "birthday gift." But she made it very clear that she was not to be called "Grandma." She said, "I'm still young to be called Grandma or Granny." By my daughter, she wished to be called "Nana." Mama spoiled her rotten. My daughter's arrival was expected a week after Mama's birthday on the 29th, but she decided to make her entrance the day after, on the 22nd.

The day Mama found out I was pregnant, there were so many emotions. I had already taken an at home test a few nights prior, before going to the doctor, but I did not tell her. I was scared. I told Mama that I needed to see our family doctor because I was having stomach pains. When my name was called, my stomach dropped. The doctor asked so many questions, and I side-eyed Mama as I answered them. Right after he exited the room, she followed him and whispered to him, "Will you give her a pregnancy test?" He replied that it was protocol for the stomach pains and symptoms I told him I was experiencing. When Mama returned to the room, I laughed and told her that I could hear her. She sucked at whispering. We both laughed.

Moments later, the doctor entered the room again, looked at me, and said, "I have good news and bad news. Which one do you want first?" I was terrified. I said, "Bad news first," because I thought it was going to be that I was pregnant. To me, it was bad news at the time, but he only told us that I was dehydrated. Then he said, "Now, the good news: You're about six weeks pregnant. I pretended to be in shock with my eyes wide open. Mama began crying and smiling at the same time, screaming, "I knew it, I knew it!" She ran out of the doctor's office and went outside so fast to make phone calls and tell everyone while she was still crying. When she came back in, I said, "Mama, that test is wrong, it's wrong," knowing it wasn't, but I was scared and now nervous. She and the doctor both asked if I wanted another test to be done to be sure, but I said no and finally told Mama the truth, because I couldn't keep it from her anymore.

The doctor asked if we would like some time to discuss options and started to explain them to us. Mama immediately shut it down and said that there were no other options to consider, because she didn't agree with terminating my pregnancy. I was scared, but she was right, and I knew better. As we walked back to the car, I was shaking. We had a very long talk as she drove us home. After she parked, we sat in the car to finish our conversation. There were family members and some of my childhood best friends already outside, waiting for our return home. They were smiling, but I wasn't.

Mama supported me through the entire pregnancy. She was not proud of the choices I had made, but she was happy to have her first grandchild arriving. Her and Dad's only request was that I finish school and graduate. She said, "I knew you was pregnant because you started gaining weight and drinking a lot of milk," which was a giveaway. It's also what made me decide to take the test—I hated milk.

During my pregnancy, Mama and I wore the same clothes sometimes, as my sister and I used to do. When I was nine months pregnant, we stood outside our apartment and took pictures together of our outfits. Mama had on a green, white, and black flower shirt, and I, a yellow, white, and black flower shirt. We both wore black capri shorts.

For reasons I can't explain (besides I loved Mama's soft bed), I slept with her during my pregnancy. She didn't mind at all. While celebrating her on the evening of her birthday, I began having pain in my back that transferred to my stomach, but I toughed it out because I didn't want to end her day. I figured it was just Braxton-Hicks contractions.

Mama and I wearing matching clothes when I
was nine months pregnant with Tommy.

The next morning before school, I woke up in Mama's bed in pain. I called to let her know what I was feeling, and she said, "Get back in bed and call the doctor to see when they can see you." I was told they could see me late in the afternoon. Mama was not OK with that. She said, "I'm getting off work and I'll take you to the hospital if you want to go." I was in so much pain, I decided to go. I was dehydrated and dilated two centimeters. After my exam, the doctor asked if I would like to be induced so that I wouldn't have to come back in the next few days to have her; I was scared. Mama looked at me and said, "It's OK, I'm right here," while nodding her head for me to have her. She agreed to stay with me. The doctor said that he was going to lunch and would like a decision once he was back. Mama was excited and ready, but I was nervous and felt unprepared, because I didn't have my hospital bag.

Mama and I decided together that it was time. She told me that it would have been OK if I needed to go to the hospital the night before, that she was ready.

Each November, Mama celebrates her niece's birthday. They shared a very close and special bond. Their times together always had laughter, dancing, and sometimes food. She loved Mama's fried pork chop; it was her favorite thing she'd make for her. They lived not too far from each other. For her niece's birthdays Mama put a huge white tent up in her yard, with tables and chairs, music playing, and food being grilled and cooked. Mama loved dancing with her, even if they were the only two. She enjoyed "shaking a tail feather," as she would call it (but today, we call it twerking).

They shared a lot more than family ties too; they shared their lives with each other and deep conversations. It was a friendship of trust and rooted in love. The relationship they shared went beyond the traditional roles of aunt and niece; it was beautiful. It was also the little things that they shared when apart. When Mama rode by her house, day or night, she made herself known to her niece by blowing the horn to let her know that it was her passing by. She always knew it was Mama.

Etta loved to dance no matter the time or day. If there was music, she was dancing. Those hips were always in motion. She drove a gray Honda Accord, and when she drove near, you would know it. She played music with the bass up just enough to feel it through her body. Surprisingly, one of her favorite artists was Lil Boosie. She would play her favorite song so loudly that you'd hear her coming up the street with "Set It Off" booming from her car while she tried her hardest to remember the lyrics. She'd be bouncing her head up and down and moving her hand in different motions to the song. It's one of the funniest things to me, because she never knew the exact words, but she enjoyed it.

Etta was also a great cook. She cooked not only for her family but for others as well. One thing I have always tried to master exactly like hers but couldn't quite get to taste the same was her cubed steaks and cabbage. She would show me the exact steps, but I just didn't like the taste. She often made spaghetti for my brother, because that was his favorite dish. Kaisha's favorite was her barbecue chicken. Mama also made the best pasta salads for almost all the family functions and events, and others would have her make it for them and their families too.

Mama and Kaisha also have this obsession with tumbler cups. She had a lot of them around the house. They were everywhere. They were in her car, at work, in her work bag, in the cabinets at home, and on the TV stand, and there were a ton in a thirty gallon storage container. The tumblers had different things on them: some with scriptures, some with animals, pictures of Grandma, the grandkids, her, her children, cartoon characters, and much more. I always wondered why they needed so many.

Chapter 4

Unexpected Love

Etta loved love. No matter what she went through, she still believed and hoped for her happy ending. She always gave love and yearned to be loved in the way she gave; she expected it back. Love has its way of finding us when we least expect it. Love has its way of changing us, whether we're ready for it or not. Love has its way of showing up in unexpected places with unexpected people. Love is love!

In 2009, Etta began to open her heart again. She welcomed a friendship with David. He was very persistent, but she was being cautious because he was no stranger to the family. We were not as open to this new friendship with him as she was. He slowly became more present in our lives as he wooed her. He started by buying nice things, especially purses and perfume, because they were her favorite. He began to show up more often, buying lunch on her breaks from work, and spending more time with her daily. Money and things were thrown at her feet.

She spoke more about him each visit, telling us how much he said he cared for her, the things he had done, the places he took her to eat, and the interesting conversations they have had. She was intrigued by the way he kept his word and showed up for her. Eventually, she decided to let her guard down and make things official with their relationship.

My siblings, Dad, and I felt that the relationship between the two was inappropriate, because he was once married to a family member that shared a bond with her when she and Dad were together. We shared our thoughts and encouraged her not to continue the relationship with him, given that it may cause issues in the family. We did not want that to happen, but she decided to go with it anyway. I felt that it was wrong at the time, but Mama was grown, and she knew what she wanted to do, regardless of our opinions or the family's.

During this time, both my siblings found out that they were expecting their babies around the same time. Sterlyng was expecting his first child, a baby boy, and Kaisha, a baby girl. We were excited and knew something was going on when Kaisha, Sterlyng's partner, and I had a girls' night that ended with them both being really sick.

David had begun to stick around more often, and sometimes even stayed at our apartment. I had a soon-to-be-two-year-old daughter, and my sister was expecting to deliver her daughter soon, so with a growing family, we needed a bigger place to live. We moved into a bigger apartment on the other side of town in Gumlog, where things slowly began to change. Some of the changes were for the better even; Mama struggled less to take care of herself and the bills, and still do for her children. She was glowing and happy.

A few months after we were settled into the new apartment, I graduated high school in May of 2010. In June, Sterlyng's son was born, and Kaisha's daughter in August. We teased them that they had planned to have children at the same time, though we knew they hadn't. Mama still said that she was too young to be called anyone's grandma and demanded to be called Nana. She was teased too because it was funny watching her face scrunch up as we asked her why and said that she wasn't getting any younger. She would say, "Nothing gets old but your clothes!"

When Kaisha was in her third trimester, we used to joke and fake that her water had broken. Mama would get excited but worried at the same time while getting ready to go to the hospital, until we'd laugh and tell her it was a joke. And then one night it wasn't. On the night that her water actually broke, Kaisha and I were watching a movie in the living room while Mama was sleeping in bed. Kaisha had gone to use the bathroom, and when she came back into the living room and started to squat down to sit on the couch, her water broke. She quickly caught herself and stood back up, went into her bedroom, and stood over a towel. I ran into Mama's room to tell her that it wasn't a joke this time: Kaisha's water broke. And she said, "Stop lying; are you for real!?"

I said, "Yes Mama, I'm for real this time." She jumped up out of bed and went to check. It was time. She called one of her close friends to take us to the hospital. My aunt met us there, and she and Mama both were by Kaisha's side as she delivered her daughter.

Etta's relationship with her grandchildren was amazing. Their bond was everything to her. She had more love to give because of them; it was deeper than you could imagine. Gentle, kind, patient. The three of us siblings were like, "Where did the Etta we knew when we were smaller go?" because we got in trouble way more than our kids did by her. She was also their safe space. My niece even called Mama her mama.

Kaisha and Etta went to Walmart or other stores literally every single day, even if they didn't specifically need anything. They would walk around just looking and spending quality time together by doing so. There wasn't much to see in our small town or places to shop, so many people would rather go out of town, but these two were perfectly fine with shopping in our area and getting food.

I moved out a few months after graduating. Mama called every day to check in and see how her grandbaby was doing. Most days, she'd come over to get her when she was off from work and say that she was giving me a break, but I knew better, she just wanted her for her.

I was also in between jobs, so Mama helped when she could. I worked at Wares BBQ, Hardees, and then McDonald's for about three months until I decided to join the Army. I had wondered about joining the military for about a year, but I kept backing out until I spoke with a recruiter to help figure out if it was best for me at that time. I was nervous about leaving my baby girl, but I knew she was in good hands with Mama. She and I went to the courthouse, I signed guardianship over to her, and I shipped out in October of 2012.

Dad, Mama, David, my daughter, my siblings, and myself all traveled to Statesboro, Georgia, for ship out day. I was heading to Military Entrance Processing Station (MEPS) for in processing. As I started signing paperwork, discussing things with the recruiter, and preparing to leave with my bags on the van, Mama disappeared. I asked everyone if they had seen where she might have gone so I could tell her that I was about to leave. Of course, I had to hug her and tell her how much I love her. Dad said, "She's probably somewhere crying!" He was right. We found her in the bathroom, crying. I told her that I was OK and I was only going to MEPS, Basic Combat Training (BCT), and Advanced Individual Training (AIT), but to her, it was like I was leaving for war. She was not convinced. Again, I reassured her that I was OK and would call and write as much as I was able to.

While in BCT at Fort Jackson, South Carolina, I cried every night for the first few weeks, missing Mama and my baby girl. Everything just seemed so hard, and having a battle buddy (someone they assign to be your partner in BCT) that was in trouble a lot made it worse, because when she was in trouble, so was I. I hated the pit. I couldn't focus from wanting to be home so badly. I began writing letters to my family and telling Mama how things were and what I was feeling. She wrote back with letters and pictures that my daughter had drawn. She would write, *She said it says "Mommy, I love you."* Mama told me everything that was happening back home, including that my sister was pregnant again. I was not able to go home for Thanksgiving, but for Christmas I did.

Hey mommy, how are you and everyone doing?

I miss you so much mama and I am so ready to see you and hear your voice. I was scared at first being here but I am doing ok, and missing regular food. When I come home, I want junk food and candy so please have me some. How is my baby girl doing? I miss her terribly and cried last night because I just thought I heard her voice. Guess I just miss her that much, huh. I sleep with her picture under my pillow every night.

Please write me as much as you can. Being here is a challenge but I won't give up mama. Thank you for taking care of my baby while I am away. I really appreciate you for doing this for me so that I can make a better life for us. I hope you have received my other letters; I know I write a lot. I went to church on Sunday, and I am finding so much joy in going, it's one of my favorite things here. I should have my phone on Sundays if we are not busy. I hope to call you and to get a letter from you soon. I love you!

Hey baby girl, I hope all is well.

Everything here has been going good. I miss you too and can't wait to have you home again. I hope you are doing ok. Tommy is doing fine. She misses her mama and says she wants to see you. She's doing really good in school also, writing her name, letters, and shapes. Everyone says hello and that they will write you; I will give them the address. Are you eating good? Are they taking care of my baby? How has things been going, tell me everything. I have been working a lot but on my off days I have been trying to get some rest when I can. I don't want you to worry about anything here at home, just do what you have to and graduate. I am so proud of you baby girl. Your dad will drive when we come to get you for Christmas. I love you and I will write you again soon, Love mama.

We weren't allowed to have our phones but for once a week for what felt like ten minutes each time. It was not enough for me, especially when I turned my phone on one night to missed texts from Mama that seemed urgent. I called right away. She told me that Sterlyng was in his car with a few friends when they had an accident, and he was in the hospital. She was so worried and brought up the fact that he often still complained about chest pain. His heart murmur closed completely while in high school, but Mama was still scared of the what ifs. I told her that I would see if I could come home. I ended the call quickly so I could turn my phone back in and ask my drill sergeant if I could go home. He expressed his thoughts and told me that I had only two weeks left until graduation. That if I left now, I wouldn't be able to come back and graduate on time, so I stayed and cried it out. I wanted to be there for him, but I couldn't be.

After nine weeks of training, in January of 2013, David drove Mama and my daughter to my graduation. We went bowling and had a great time together while I told them all about the training we had done. Mama told me how proud she was of me and how much she loved me. She shared many little stories of my daughter and the silly things she did and said. She also showed me more pictures Tommy had colored and drawn. After a few hours of eating and enjoying our time together, it was time to return for accountability. I couldn't go home with them because I was shipping out to AIT from there.

While in AIT at Fort Lee, Virginia, I was happy to have my phone. I talked to Mama as much as I could, because I felt like giving up and coming home so many times. She encouraged me to stay and keep pushing. I remember having my last physical training test and aiming for max. I ran as fast and hard as I could, because I was beating my record every time, and maxing was the only thing I hadn't done yet. When I crossed the finish line, my instructor called out my run time: I missed max by four seconds, and I cried. I got back to my room and called Mama while crying. She thought something bad had happened, but it was just those four seconds that I was upset about. She said, "It's OK, Domanique, you passed didn't you? That's all that matters." I was so upset about it and just needed to hear her voice to calm me down. It did, and she continued to encourage me to keep going.

After graduating AIT in March of 2013, I went home for two weeks, enjoyed time with my family, and attended my cousin's wedding before going to my very first duty station at Fort Campbell, Kentucky, in April. During this time, I drove home a lot to visit and spend time with everyone, because I struggled with being away from my family. I had never been away before, but over time, I became more comfortable with the change. It was also around this time that Sterlyng had his appearance in court for the vehicle accident. He was unfortunately sent to spend time away in a penitentiary. Etta was devastated.

While he was away, it took a lot from Mama. She kept her children close as possible. She talked with us every day to know of our well-being and to tell us that she loved us, but now she couldn't do that with him away. It broke her heart. She stressed herself about seeing him every chance she could, to put eyes on him for herself and make sure that he was OK. Thankfully, she had a particularly good relationship with her coworkers, and they worked with her to be able to take time off on weekends for visitations as much as she needed to see him. Mama didn't skip a visit unless he was further away or something was going on that prevented her from going. When I visited Mama, Kaisha and I traveled with her often to see him. We even took the kids sometimes. I could see upon her face just how much seeing him made some of her worries depart. Her face would light up so bright as she hugged and scanned him from head to toe with her eyes, but he never noticed. All we wanted was for him to stay focused and out of trouble, and to return home safely.

Mama and Sterlyng

To my special lady on Mother's Day,

Thinking of you today and praying God blesses your day and fills it with many reminders of how much he loves you and wants to bless you. Have A Happy Mother's Day.

I want you to know that I love you so much!

Love, Sterlyng

Hi, my love, my baby boy,

I hope all is well and that I will be able to come see you this week. It was so good to see you on Saturday as always, and I hope and pray to God that this will all be over sooner than we think. All I have to say is to follow your heart son, but always keep your mind, body, and soul on God because he will never leave you or forsake you. I had a dream about you. You were home where you belong.

I was happy to receive a letter and Mother's Day card from you. Faith is all we need. I am hoping you will be home before Christmas so we can all have a peace of mind, but God is in control, and he will get us back where we need to be. Son, mom loves you more than you will ever know. You are my one and only son. I will never let you down, just keep doing right and stay away from trouble. You are a loving wonderful young man that made a bad turn, but God has already made some turns for you. I see the change in you and that's so wonderful to have that feeling. God is always in control. Prayer changes things, not only in you, but things have changed in me also, not just because of what happened. This is just a test. I am closing my letter but never ever my love for you. Until next time, peace and be still!!!

Lord, I ask in your name that you give my loving son your Wisdom, Knowledge, and Understanding.

In the name of Jesus, Amen!
Love mommy

Chapter 5

The Evolution of Us

I enjoyed going back home to visit, but sometimes I wished I had stayed away. In the beginning things were good, and we all enjoyed each other's company. We did things together like cooking and grilling, going to small family functions, and taking the kids to the park, and David would even write little notes on cards that Mama sent to Sterlyng. We still had opinions about their relationship, but we became a family. Each visit was different in some way. There were little things I picked up on here and there that caught my attention, but nothing to worry about, I thought.

In any relationship, there are disagreements; however, it's how you choose to handle those moments that means the most. Communication and respect are important. The disagreements between Mama and David were mostly small. Every so often he would ask for our opinions on them or share some things we thought were inappropriate for us to even have an opinion on. This happened often, but we didn't always feel the need to respond, because it wasn't our place in their relationship.

Things were going well, even with the disagreements, until alcohol entered the picture. As the amount David consumed increased over time, the arguments got worse. Often, David would encourage each of us to drink along with him, because he didn't want to drink alone. Mama was not a heavy drinker, nor did she drink the same beverages or drink as often as he did, but she did partake. She had plans to completely stop soon.

We had never dealt with anyone that consumed alcohol as often or as much as David did, so we didn't know what it looked like or what to look for in terms of behavior changes—if we should even be on the lookout for any. With alcohol came a few small arguments and petty disagreements, but nothing that couldn't be hugged out later. That was, until the alcohol intake picked up. The small arguments and disagreements turned into awful verbal fights, and shortly after those started, I noticed David began bringing his firearm into the house after work. He had been driving trucks for years. To my understanding, he had the firearm for safety reasons as he drove, but he would bring it home so that it wouldn't get stolen from the truck while he was away. This caught me by surprise, because I did not expect that Mama would be OK with a weapon like that around in the house.

I had mixed feelings about it. I had my own thoughts about what could happen but was not afraid of the what ifs. I was worried about the weapon being in the house now that we could visually see the changes in his moods the more he consumed, and of the unknown it could bring.

I spoke with Kaisha on multiple occasions about my concerns, and she shared hers. After one of these talks, I decided to have a conversation about our concerns with Mama. We spoke over the phone, and she assured me everything was OK and that he safely put his weapon away once he returned home. For me, the issue was not that he had a weapon; it was that he would show it off. I don't know why he did it, but oftentimes he would show it and ask us to hold it or to see how the weight of it felt in our hands. I also noticed that it was not always secured properly; it was just tucked under something if it was not on his hip.

My concerns grew when he got upset over things. There were a few times he'd hold it in his hand or place it in the holster on his hip when he got upset, but he never used it. As Etta's children, we worried for Mama's safety when we were not around and made sure to call and check in with her as often as we could. She never expressed any concerns or issues of her own, but I'm sure there were some she kept to herself. Mama did not like confrontations at all and tended to stay quiet on things.

Etta found out that her oldest sister had breast cancer, and on top of everything she already had going, she immediately wanted to know what she could do to help. She made sure to call, text, and show up to see her sister when she could. Her goal was to be the glue and keep everyone together after Grandma Johnnie had died. Breast cancer was such a shock to us all, but Mama stayed positive. She kept a smile on her face, worked her normal shifts caring for her residents, took care of her family, and made sure everyone knew how much she cared for and loved them.

She carried on as if all things were good, but her children and grandchildren were affected by the growing changes and behaviors of her relationship.

I began to develop anxiety.

I found out that I was pregnant again in November of 2015. I was happy and emotional at the same time when I called and told Mama; she was the first to know. She was excited. She told me how she hoped it was a boy, and if so, I would know from how the pregnancy went. She was right, it was a boy. It was completely different from my first pregnancy. With my daughter, it was a breeze with the only issue being dehydration. But with my son, it was a challenge.

I felt something was wrong with the pregnancy but didn't know what until I blacked out at work. I was working in the kitchen and serving on the line while the heat and steam from the serving line brushed against my face. I felt weak. I decided I needed a break and to drink some water. I sat down in a booth and moments later was woken up by a coworker asking if I was feeling OK. I said yes, but I knew something was off, because it happened again. So, I went to the doctor for some tests. The doctor told me that I was Rh-negative and may not carry to term. I panicked and called Mama.

She prayed and helped me through my pregnancy. I was personally having a hard time with things already. I prayed for my son and wasn't going to let anything happen to him. I knew that God had the last say so, so I kept my faith. The doctors agreed that it wasn't safe for me to be alone or to drive due to the blackouts, but I realized that only heat brought them about. My unit moved me to work at the company until I gave birth in July of 2016 and returned to work. Mama was a little disappointed that she wasn't there for the birth of my son, but she came right away to make sure that we were well.

She was proud of me breastfeeding. She encouraged it and told me, "I tried it, but it hurt, so I stopped." We laughed about it because her facial expression was like she could still feel the pain of one of us biting her. I breastfed for a year. When we visited Mama, my son would often get hungry while she was holding him. He would grab at her shirt, and she would laugh saying, "Ain't no milk in here, Domanique come and get him!" It was the funniest thing to see.

David and my son grew close to each other. He was really excited to see David and Mama as he got older each year. They spent a lot of time together playing when we were home. David watched as my son took his first few steps, tried different foods, and learned to talk. It seemed to be a joy to have him around and things seemed to be a little better than before. There were less disagreements and everyone was getting along well, until late one evening, when there was a fight.

A few of us were gathered on Mama's front porch with a friend of the family, discussing detailing our cars as we often did. David arrived home as we were talking. He parked his car and walked toward the porch. As he walked by us, we smelled a bit of alcohol. For whatever reason, he began questioning the guy about why he was there and told him he could leave. Jokingly, as he always did, the guy said, "I don't have to go anywhere!" Everyone was quiet. Immediately, David got angry and started arguing with the guy. Then suddenly, he began physically fighting with him and tossed him across the railing of the porch. He stormed into the house and went into the bedroom. When he came back into view, we saw that he had grabbed his weapon, cocked it, and was walking toward the front door. I stepped in between him and the door and tried to calm him down. I told him to put it away because our children were present and afraid.

He didn't seem to care about what I was saying. He shouted at me, said that I was picking sides, and that the weapon was not loaded. It did not matter in that moment if the weapon was loaded or not; it should have never been pulled out, especially in front of the children. I was concerned for our safety. This was the first time I thought he was actually going to hurt someone and did not care about us or our children. We had never seen this side of him before, and we didn't like it. He wasn't perfect, but this was too much. It was the beginning of his deeper alcohol issues, which we were not aware of.

Time usually helps things get better, but for David, it was not on his side. The more time went by, the more alcohol he consumed. It was like water. With that came more arguments and fights like clockwork, and it was unhealthy for us all, but we got used to it.

I had received news that I would be moving back to Georgia and was happy about this, because I wanted to be closer to Mama now more than ever. When I called and gave her the news, she was so excited.

In early 2019, after ten years of Mama and David's relationship, I began having very disturbing, vivid, and horrible nightmares. I had the same dreams repeatedly of him, my brother, and me. We ran through the back street of the Racetrack apartments we first lived in, with firearms in our hands, looking for him as he was looking for us. It was like we were hunting. My brother and I chased him in the field where there once was a playground and fired toward him, and he returned fire toward us each time. Sometimes in my dreams he would catch up and shoot me. Then other times, we caught up to him first, but with each dream, at least one of us died. I could see and feel these dreams as if they were happening in real life. Sometimes I could see myself watching it play out as a movie, and other times I would be in it: I could look down and see my chest, hands, legs, and feet. It disturbed me.

I told Dad about the dreams but not quite all the details, just that I had bad dreams about David sometimes that really bothered me. He asked if I had talked with Mama about them, and I told him yes, but I didn't know for sure if she took them as seriously as I did, because to me they feel like a warning. I told him that I didn't know what else to do. Dad said that he hoped one day she would leave David and come home if she needed to, or just leave him and move on with her life.

Mom and Dad didn't have any dealings together outside of us after their split, but he always held on to her in some way. It hurt him to see getting her heart broken time after time. He moved on with his life throughout the years, but he never fully let her go. He still loved (and loves) the mother of his children and would have done anything for her. It's an unexplainable unconditional kind of love that can't be broken.

After our talk, I opened another conversation with Mama about my concerns and dreams. I had this bad feeling that one day something horrible was going to happen if she didn't let this relationship go. It was a constant feeling I just could not shake. She did not say much on the matter or show much acknowledgement of the issue when I brought it up to her, but I know she understood where I was coming from. She chose not to speak on my dreams, but I wanted to make sure she knew that I was here no matter what. There were other occasions that I would ask if things were going OK. She said things were fine but I knew she kept things to herself so we wouldn't worry about her, but of course we did anyway.

To ease my mind about her safety, I often tried to convince Mama to visit me in Virginia for a few days or so before I moved. I also wanted to show her that there was more to the world than just our hometown and work. I told her she could relax, take her mind off things, see and do things she had not done yet, and enjoy herself away from the troubles at home. In April, she was ready to visit. I couldn't drive to Georgia to pick her up because I had things going on at the time with work, so she agreed to fly. Mama had never flown on a plane before; she was nervous.

When she made it into the airport, I was so excited. I was

already waiting on her at baggage claim and so happy to see her once she turned the corner. She had the biggest smile on her face as she walked toward me with open arms and hugged me. While walking out of the airport to the car, she explained how scared and nervous she was on the plane. Mama said that there was a lady sitting next to her on the plane and they talked. She helped her feel a little more comfortable about the flight.

My daughter was on a field trip that day, so Mama and I enjoyed our alone time and caught up as I showed her around. I wanted to surprise my daughter with her Nana's visit, so I didn't tell her she was coming. When we picked Tommy up from school that afternoon, Mama stayed in the car smiling, and she was even more excited than I was to be there. Tommy walked closer to the car. I could see her trying to peep and see who was sitting on the passenger side. Before she got into the car, she realized it was Mama and was shocked. She smiled and asked, "Nana, how did you get here?" The next few days, Tommy asked to skip school and stay home, but I only let her stay the first day. They were glued to each other for the rest of the visit.

In June, I relocated my daughter back to our hometown to enjoy her summer as she usually did with family and also to ad-just, because I was soon moving to Hunter Army Airfield base in Georgia. She began school that August and continued to live with her grandmother.

Sterlyng was released and returned home in August. I was not home to see him, but I made sure he knew that I would as soon as I moved. He was in prison for five years, then transferred to a halfway house for a year before getting out. While he was in the halfway house, he had a cell phone, so we could call. We drove often to spend time with him or bring him back to Mama's house for a few hours until he had to return for the night. His transition went well. He was able to go to job interviews, make money for himself before getting home, and see the different things that had changed while he was gone.

Mama was so happy to have her baby boy home. She made sure that he knew how proud of him she was and that he had everything he needed for his return home. He was able to fall back into things at a slow but steady pace. He gained his independence, began working on the road with our uncle, and moved into a home in the country. His house was where we often got together as a family to enjoy one another's presence. He had a big yard that we would gather in for holidays, to grill, and have the children's birthday parties.

Before his release, Kaisha and I shared our concerns about Mama and David's relationship. We hoped that everything would continue going smoothly, so Sterlyng wouldn't have to see the changes. His transition and making sure he stayed home, out of trouble, and safe were very important. This was the most crucial time for him. We did not need him getting into things with Mama's relationship, as we were brought into them. Sterlyng and David grew a bond. They went on a few trips to the racetrack, enjoyed time alone to talk, and caught up with each other on things Sterlyng had missed.

Chapter 6

The Holidays

Thanksgiving was just a few weeks away when my son and I relocated. Mama was so excited to have us home. We moved into her house for a month or so while I was on leave from the Army to spend time with family and find housing. She told me to stay as long as I needed. She cooked almost every day, and it spoiled me; I did not want to leave, nor was I having much luck searching for houses online. I found a few I was interested in seeing in person, so I asked Mama to go house hunting with me. She agreed to go and we went on her days off from work. I figured it would be fun to do together and she would help me make the final decision.

We walked through a few houses and apartment buildings, but we were not really excited about them. I took another scroll online for houses in the area while we were at lunch. There were three houses we saw in the same neighborhood that caught our attention. Mama said the layouts of the first two were weird. I loved the windows, but we kept looking. Before leaving the second house, I tried opening the slide door to the kitchen to view the backyard, but the door came off the hinges. Mama and I looked at each other and laughed. She said, "Let's get out of here before they think we're tearing up their house." I propped the door back up and we quickly left.

The third house was on the next street over. It was nice with a fenced-in backyard, which was something I wanted that the other houses didn't have. As we walked through, Mama repeated that she liked it and she thought I should get it. She was happy about this house. I honestly liked it as well. As we were leaving, another car pulled up with people who wanted to view the house. Mama looked at me and said, "Call the people right now before it's gone." I did.

Etta assisted on picking out furniture and other things I needed in my new home, because there were a few things I left behind when I moved.

After my son and I were settled in, I visited home, which was now about an hour and a half away, almost every weekend. Mama was happy to have us near home again. I believe having us around really made her feel better; it kept her from worrying about us as all mothers do.

She always had a room for me and the kids to come home to. When we were staying with her, she sometimes poked her head in the door or came in the room for no reason at all, just to talk. Most days she got home from work after 4 p.m. and still cooked meals for us. She'd play catch with my son with a small ball she bought from a nearby store. They played catch every day; it was their thing and he loved it. There was so much joy and love in her voice while we were staying with her. Even if she was tired, she made sure to be present in those moments with us.

Nightmares turned into terrors. I was more than worried; I felt afraid. Not of him and what he may have been capable of, but of the way I felt after each dream. Each dream felt extremely real and they had begun to take a toll on my mind, body, and spirit. I even felt on edge when David continued to ask for our opinions on the simple disagreements he and Mama had. I ignored him as much as I could, because we never knew what mood or state of mind he was in. I often wondered when "it" would happen, whatever "it" was, and to whom and how exactly. Would there ever be change? Were the nightmares a warning of what was to come if things did not change? Were we safe? Just David's presence alone affected others in one way or another, even the children. Disagreements lead to being called disrespectful names; speaking on our relationships, children, and things he claimed he didn't like about us; and being verbally abusive. However, when things were going well, we were highly praised for the exact same things, told how much he loved us, and that he would never hurt us. We appreciated the highs, but they left us confused.

After things quieted down a bit or it was the following day and we'd collected ourselves, David offered us things. It was money, food, or other things to try and settle us, and it worked a lot in the beginning, but I began to see the patterns. Eventually, we stopped accepting things as peace offerings from him, and we could tell he noticed it didn't work as well as it used to, but he continued trying anyway.

Occasionally, we would have conversations with David about things he said or did that bothered us. For example, one time when my son was two or three years old, we were all sitting in the living room as a family, having a good time laughing, talking, watching TV, and making jokes, as we did. David was in the bedroom watching TV with the door open. My son was to himself, riding his tricycle up and down the hallway from the living room to where Mama's bedroom was. I was sitting near the hallway on the loveseat when David came storming out the room. He snatched my son by one arm off the tricycle and said, "I'm trying to watch TV." I immediately went off and demanded he put my son down and give the bike back. And I told him that he would not touch my son again.

It seemed as if whatever David was going through was taken out on my son, because the tricycle barely made any noise. And if anything, we were the ones being very loud, so he should have told us to quiet down instead.

Whenever stuff like this happened, the next day David would say he couldn't remember, blame it on everyone else, or dismiss the whole thing, so we would agree to leave it alone. This upset me, because not only did it feel dismissive, but I also felt that, drinking or not, he knew what he was doing. As it continued to happen, and he came with the same excuses, it didn't take long to realize that he was not going to change.

Sterlyng, Kaisha, I, and our kids grew a love-hate relationship toward him. What happened to the "Good Guy" we all knew and loved? I hated this. It caused broken relationships, friendships, and family relations.

Christmas was Etta's favorite time of the year. The closer it got, the more excited she got. Each year it was a huge thing for her, and we enjoyed every minute of it. When we were growing up, on Christmas Eve before bed, she told each of us that we could open one present. We were so excited as she stood over us smiling and watching, so proud at what she was able to do for us to make us happy. We got toys, clothes, socks, and underwear. Mama always bought Kaisha and me matching clothes to wear to school until we were in middle school. Sometimes the colors would be different, but the outfits were the exact same. In the beginning we loved it, but as we got older and fought more, as siblings do, we began to hate it. Sterlyng's gifts were often cologne, wallets, or boxers, and he loved big trucks and Hot Wheels cars. He would open them and run outside to bring in sticks to break into little logs so he could play as if he was hauling them, like Dad did. He had tractors and other things surrounding that helped load and unload them at a "mill" he made up. Then he snuck into Mama's nail polish for the Hot Wheels.

He used nail polish to paint his cars at his "paint shop." All the cars would have a new set of rims and a paint job. You could smell the nail polish throughout the house while he painted them and set them out to dry. Kaisha and I loved playing with him. We even pretended to have our own church going in our bedroom, and he would beat the drums he had gotten one year for Christmas. It was our thing, especially if we heard the church music from the nearby church.

One year, we got a Nintendo 64. We hooked it up to our TV, which was on top of a dresser next to our bedroom door, and we played the game. Our parents were in the living room with family members. Suddenly, a rat ran across the floor next to me and I yelled. When Mom and Dad noticed what was going on, I cussed at the rat. I said, "That motherf***** is gone!" Everyone was in shock as they looked around at each other. Then they all burst out in laughter. Thankfully, I didn't get in trouble because they found it so funny at the time. I still hear about that day even now.

While Mama had her rough patches in the early years after she and Dad split, Sterlyng used to do what he could to make sure

Christmas was always fun and that we received presents. I don't know how he did it those years, but he did. One year he tried to do our hair before giving us presents. He put our hair in sideways, frizzy ponytails with bows, but we appreciated it. Then, he gave us both camouflage purses. Kaisha's was brown and mine was blue.

Now that we have our own children, we carry on the Christmas Eve gift opening with them. We also included Mama each year. When Mama had to work on Christmas Day, we waited until she arrived home to open them, but the kids were not so patient, so we took them to receive their gifts from family and friends and found other things to do in the meantime.

Etta loved seeing her children and grandchildren together, destroying the house with gift wrapping paper and toys every-where as we opened presents. No matter how old we were, she still bought presents for us. As we got older, she sometimes gave them to us early. She'd buy things that we needed, like kitchen tools and household things, or give us money. Watching the way her face lit up with her smile and laughter was everything. She was proud of herself for getting the kids things that they wanted and embracing the blessing of us all. She would ask the kids if they were happy as they hugged her and said, "Thank you, Nana!" Then David would give us all money, because he didn't really buy gifts unless they were for Mama.

Buying gifts for Mama was fairly easy. Usually, her gifts were things she wanted often, like perfume or a nice-sized purse. She was not a fan of smaller bags, because she carried so much in them and needed the space. We used to mess with her and tell her that we were going to get her something different for Christmas or her birthday even though that wasn't what she preferred. Though if we did, she was always grateful and accepting of the things we purchased or made personally for her.

New Year's Day was more chilled and relaxed as a family. The night before, Mama would make sure to have the house sparkling clean: all clothes were washed, dried, and put away; floors swept and mopped; dishes cleaned; black-eyed peas and greens were cooked. And then she waited for the clock to strike twelve. If we were not at her house, she'd call each of us and other family members to say Happy New Year and to tell us how much she loved us. Then she'd head to bed right after. It wasn't just New Year's Day that she called right at 12 a.m. On our birthdays she did the exact same thing every year, never missed. Etta made sure to be the first to wish us a happy birthday and express her love for us. We looked forward to it every year, because we knew it was coming. If there were a time in which she couldn't reach us, she texted to tell us.

After the new year of 2021 there were a few changes. We spent more weekends in the country at my brother's house than at Mama's. He had a huge yard and more space than the four of us for gatherings and parties for the kids, as well as other things that would keep them entertained and busy. The kids loved the country and being out in the yard, freely enjoying themselves or playing with the dogs out back. Across the dirt road from Sterlyng's house was some land with horses fenced in. They were very calm, and I used to wonder if I could ride on them but never asked since I was honestly a little nervous to do it. Sterlyng and I used to try and teach my sister and daughter how to drive while Mama just watched and shook her head. She was too scared of their driving, saying we were too silly and heavy footed. The kids would ride their bikes and four-wheelers or jump on the trampoline. We really enjoyed ourselves.

Sterlyng's house was like our getaway from town. There was always laughter, food, games, and of course, Mama twerking when the music was on. For Easter, we planned an Easter egg hunt for the kids with maybe one hundred or more eggs, plus golden ones with money in them. A lot of the eggs were easy to find, because my son was still the baby of the group. Kaisha helped him find as many as she could, and the older kids were mainly looking for the money eggs, of course.

I also took the time to surprise Mama with a canvas that I had made for her of Grandma. I had ordered and received it two weeks before I gave it to her, but I had not been home, and wanted to give it to her in person. We were all standing in the kitchen when I told her I had something for her. She smiled and asked, "What is it?" I went into the room to get it and told her to close her eyes as I unboxed and unwrapped it. I told her to hold her hands out and placed it in her hands facing toward her. When I told her to open her eyes, I started recording and taking pictures as I expected her to have a big reaction. She cried. She asked, "When did you get this—thank you!" She hugged me while still crying and turning red. She held on to the canvas tightly and just stood stiffly, staring at it as if Grandma was looking back at her and they were sharing a moment. Mama stared and stared; she cried, and stared some more. She was silent. I knew her heart was happy, but I couldn't tell what she was feeling and thinking in that moment. It looked like peace.

In May, Mama made plans to see my son graduate Pre-K and to celebrate his accomplishments and moving on to kindergarten the following year. She traveled to Savannah the day before to attend the ceremony and spend some time with us. She was so proud and supportive no matter how big or small things were for us and the grandchildren. This was one of the many reasons we celebrated her as much as we could, especially on Mother's Day.

That Mother's Day, Mama wanted seafood, so we decided to

have a seafood boil in my brother's backyard. Instead of cooking, we all pitched in to buy seafood bags from OD Seafood in Savannah. I picked the food up that day before traveling to Swainsboro. Dad gathered with us to celebrate her. I'd missed that.

When we were all together as a family, there was always chaos, but in a good way. We're country folk. We're either being loud or picking at one another. Taking pictures was always a hassle, especially with Sterlyng and Kaisha. They would pick each other apart, or me, at the most inconvenient times, especially during pictures. Innocent sibling love language. There were plenty laughs while Mama and I yelled, "Come on now and act right!" Most photos taken caught the laughs, smiles, and our dysfunctional family. There were always good vibes.

There were a few nights we hung out in the country and David joined, and there were also times when we had no intention to invite him. We were not as inviting by then due to his past actions. With him around, it felt like we had to be on guard all the time or worried about how much he had to drink that day.

One night, everyone was gathered and having a great time together. David was not with us in the beginning of the night but walked to my brother's to join us later. The music was going while we played Uno and spades. Mama sat back and watched. She smiled, had a few laughs, did a twerk or two, and enjoyed our time together. As the night went on, a small disagreement began between Sterlyng and Kaisha. They were going back and forth as I tried to deescalate the situation, but for some reason, David decided to join in on the matter and made it worse. He added in some unnecessary things he felt about my sister's son.

When he had arrived, we could smell that he was already intoxicated, so I knew it was going to become a problem and the fun would come to an end early. It was an expected part of things with him. He and Kaisha began arguing, and he walked toward her fussing and cursing. They continued arguing but now even closer to each other's faces. Kaisha pushed him away from her, and he raised up as if to hit her. My brother and I ran to come in between and separate them, and then all hell broke loose. The first physical fight.

Sterlyng let David know that he would *not* be in Kaisha's face and speaking to her like that again. Mama yelled for us to get ahold of ourselves and to stop, but we continued. The next thing I saw was David pinned to the door. It was like I blacked out, and I began fighting with him as well. Then, the three of us ended up on the floor in front of the door somehow. In the midst of the fighting, I wanted to make sure there was no weapon on him, and if there was, I would take it, but there wasn't any I could see or feel. As I got up from the floor, Mama ran outside crying. I ran out behind her.

After the fight was over, David tried to approach Mama and talk with her. She was so upset she wouldn't speak. She couldn't catch her breath and began having a panic attack. My nephew's mother and I went outside to try and calm her and told her to sit down. I felt so bad, but we were here now and had to face it. There was so much built up that seemed to boil over, and it just happened.

I can honestly say that this fight felt good to have.

Once Mama was calm, I told her I didn't feel comfortable with her going home that night, and she agreed. My brother and I helped her into my car and drove to my house with Sterlyng trailing behind. David didn't know where I lived exactly, nor was he welcomed there, which I'm sure he knew by then. As we were on the road, he called Mama's phone many times; it annoyed her, so she decided to turn it off. Once we made it to my house, we sat up for a bit and talked, played cards again, and then went to bed.

The next morning, Sterlyng woke up early to go to work, and Mama and I slept in until she was ready to leave. David was not home. As we walked through and check the house, she noticed he had punched holes in her bedroom door from the inside of the room. It made her upset all over again, and she silently shook her head.

David returned shortly after our arrival and immediately began fussing again, because Mama still wasn't ready to talk about everything that had happened. He yelled about Sterlyng and about how we were a problem to him, how much he didn't like us, and that he would end my brother's life. I was confused, because he inserted himself into that disagreement last night, not anyone else.

Everything happened so fast after that. My sister called Dad; he and his partner rushed over. Mom called our cousin to come pick me up because I was so upset. There was no talking me down after threatening my brother's life, and there was no way I was leaving her there with him anyway. Everyone was outside yelling and screaming at one another; he continued with the threats. Then Dad said that he would not stand by as David threatened his son's life. David then went on to threaten Dad's life. Dad laughed. His partner was not happy about the threat and had a few words of her own while trying to help keep me calm at the same time. It was a mess.

At some point he walked toward Mama, yelling in her face and calling her names. She looked nervous standing there on the porch. She backed up a little but stood her ground. He continued yelling and called her a bitch, and she replied, "Well, if I'm a bitch I'm a good one and you like it!" I tried my best to get away from being held back, because I felt I needed to protect her. I thought he might hit her. At this point, I didn't care about anything but her; nothing else mattered. The altercation didn't stop until the police were called, but by the time they arrived, David had already left in his car. The disrespect was so unreal, especially toward Mama.

David slowly but surely stopped going to work; he consumed even more alcohol than before, didn't help Mama around the house, nor pick up after himself. It sucked to see Mama doing everything as soon as she came home from work. He had gin placed at his side on the coffee table with a shot glass next to the couch, which was where he mostly slept. He complained to me sometimes that Mama wouldn't lay with him. I didn't want to hear that or anything else he shared of their relationship. It was inappropriate, plus I completely understood why she wasn't.

Summer came around. Sterlyng moved from his home in the country to a house in town about a block away from Mama. Soon after, she moved from her apartment to a house across the street from his, and then Kaisha moved in two houses down from her a few months later. They were all on the same street, close to one another. Sterlyng felt that this was right, this was where mama needed to be: somewhere close so that he could keep an eye on things and be there if she needed him.

Tommy moved in with my mother. She had been staying with her other grandmother, but she had passed away. Tommy asked to continue living closer to family, so I told her that she could stay for a while but would move home with me soon, because I was preparing for the three of us to move back to Fort Campbell in December. I wasn't fully comfortable with this arrangement—her staying with Mama—because of how I felt about David, but she and Mama were excited, so I allowed it. Mama assured me that everything was alright. Also, I needed the extra help as a single parent of two, and Mama was always willing.

We talked nearly every day. Sometimes Tommy would share things about Mama and David. Often, it was about how he would say things to Mama that made her upset, but she would ignore him with a blank look on her face as if she didn't hear him, and then continue whatever she was doing in that moment.

Etta and Tommy spent a lot of quality time together. They often got their nails done at KZ Nails and ate at Ware's BBQ and Koiya, and they loved shopping. Mama also supported her while cheering when I couldn't be there. Tommy loved cheering and taking pictures. She took a lot of pictures and recorded literally everything, especially off guards. Sometimes she taught Mama TikTok dances as she recorded, and Mama would start dancing in them with her. These two loved the camera and making each other laugh; I would say that was their favorite thing about each other. Mama even taught Tommy how to two step. One night, she cleared her coffee table from the middle of the living room floor, turned on some old music, and grabbed Tommy by the hands. They danced together as the song played and I recorded. Watching them dance and enjoy that moment made my heart smile.

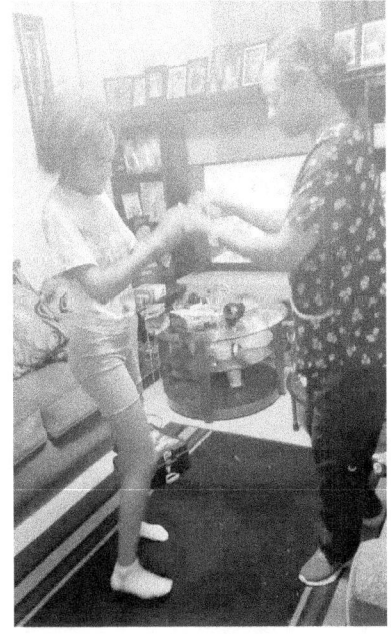

There were many mornings my daughter would miss the bus, and it so happened to be on days Mama had off from work. She would call me upset and fussing after dropping her off, saying she felt Tommy did it on purpose because she didn't like riding the bus. Mama liked to sleep in on her off days. On my end, I would laugh a little, because Mama was hardly ever upset and rarely said no to anyone, so when she fussed it sounded so funny. She'd even curse a little sometimes, especially if it was raining, but it sounded weird coming from her mouth. That was the funniest thing to see and hear. When it rained, she stayed home, and if she was in the car, she'd sit there until it slowed down or stopped. She hated getting wet.

In October, I found out that I had made the promotion list for Staff Sergeant and would be pinned in November. The first thing I thought of was thanking God, because I had been fighting for this for a while. I also wanted to ask mom to pin me. It was going to be the first time she would see me get promoted in person. I had to have her do it. I called her and we made plans for her to attend my unit's potluck where awards and promotions were presented.

There were games, competitions, and other exciting things going on. I was happy that Mama was able to attend for the first time. She and Tommy drove to Fort Stewart for my promotion. She even wore an Army shirt that day. She was proud to have the opportunity to pin me. She stood by my side as First Sergeant and my battle buddy spoke on my behalf, while holding on to my patrol cap with my new rank on it. After they finished, Mama stood in front of me smiling and seemed a bit nervous. She began by changing the rank on my chest. As she attached the new rank, she firmly pressed it against my chest twice to make sure it stuck, then proceeded to swap out my old cap with the new one. I laughed because when she put it on, it felt like it wasn't on right, so I helped her fix it.

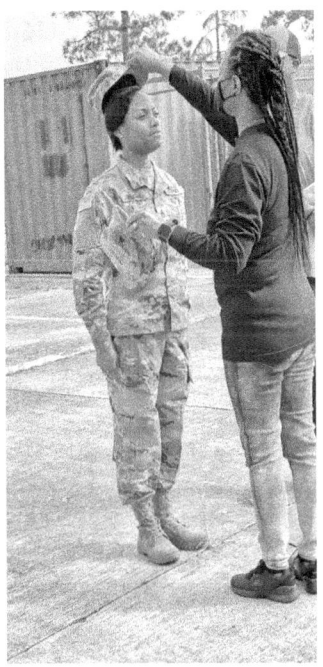

Mama placing a new cap on my head for my
promotion from Sergeant to Staff Sergeant

Mama, Tommy, my son, and I after the promotion ceremony

childhood notes to mama.

Dear Mom (Etta),

On this special day, I want to give you the best love from me that you ever had. I promise to do whatever it is to make you happy. When I was born, I was just a little baby, but you brought me from there to a 12 year old girl who love you very, very, very much with all my heart for raising me up to be who I am today. It feels good to me to have a mother that understands me more than any other do, you are a mother of love, I can set beside you now and talk to you and you will listen even if it takes an hour.

＿＿﹀＿﹍

I love you with all my heart.

＿＿﹀＿﹍

We are in things together through hard time or easy times.

＿＿﹀＿﹍

Der mom, it been a sweet sweet Sunday. I hope you have a good time.

＿＿﹀＿﹍

You are the woman that well let us do anything we whant to do.

＿＿﹀＿﹍

You are speial and I like that love mom.

＿＿﹀＿﹍

Mom you are so sweet that I could eat you up, not for reall.

— — ～ ﹀ ⌣

Mom, when I first saw you I'll all ready new there was something in side of you some thing that I thought that I would never finde angle of minde. I look at you looking at me now I no why thay say the best thing of breath. Gunna love you boy you are so finde angle of minde.

Family photo of us all together with our
Guardian Angel watching over us.

Mama when she was a teenage girl

Mama with her children: Sterlyng, Kaisha, and Domanique

Mama and me, downtown Hinesville, GA

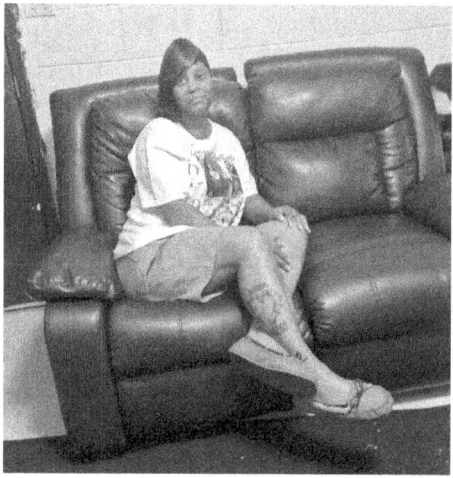

Mama sitting at Kaisha's house on her birthday

Mama standing outside her apartment

Mama at her sister's house spending time with her niece

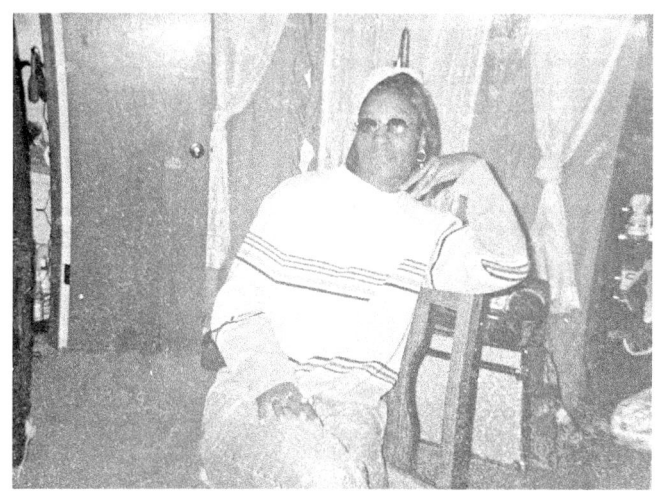

Mama visiting her brother and family

Mama enjoying time at the park with her grandkids

Mama and Kaisha at the water fountain

Chapter 7

Temporary Peace and Goodbyes

I was excited about turning thirty and I wanted to do something different for myself for once. In March of 2022, I planned a girls' trip to a cabin in Blue Ridge, Georgia. Mama, Kaisha, my brother's then-partner, my aunt, and my cousin all joined me. Etta was excited because it was something she had never done before, and I was proud to be able to continue doing things for her she'd never experienced, even the smaller things. We all wanted to drive up together, so we agreed to rent a passenger van. The morning of the trip, we gathered at Mama's house and took a few photos. My cousin had white customized T-shirts with red sayings on them made for each of us. Mine said "Dirty 30"; hers was "The Goofy Cousin"; Kaisha's, "The Drunk Sister"; Sterlyng's partner, "The Stoned Sister-in-Law"; my aunt's, "The Lit Auntie"; and Mama's said, "The Cool Mom." We grabbed food, then headed to Statesboro to pick up the van and get going. Music played the entire five-hour drive. Every so often, Mama yelled from the back: "I got to use the bathroom; I took a water pill." We'd all laugh and find a stop to stretch our legs, grab snacks, and get gas.

Once we made it to Blue Ridge, we stopped quickly at the grocery store before heading up the mountain to the cabin. Being that we were already behind on the time we wanted to arrive, we didn't want to have to go back into town later. It began to get dark out while driving up the mountain. We were all a bit nervous, even a little scared, but I tried not to show it, because I was driving. I could hear Mama and my aunt saying that I was probably OK with the drive up because I've driven in other conditions in the military. They were right, but it reminded me of the time I drove while at National Training Center (NTC) a few years before. I was nervous then too.

When we finally arrived and got inside the cabin, we immediately fell in love. We explored what we could as the evening grew into night. While I was recording around the cabin, Mama was walking around excited and smiling as big as she could, saying, "This is nice!"

She walked into the camera's view, and I told her, "Ma, say hey!"

She looked into the camera and said, "Heyyyy," dragging it out as if she was talking to a baby. We both laughed. Her glow told me how she was feeling in that moment: She was excited to be there. We all enjoyed some time and laughter together before finding our rooms and settling in for the night. Mama and I shared a room. It felt like old times again. We shared a few things with each other and talked about the plans I had for us while playing games on our phones. She loved Word Search. She played it all night until she got sleepy. Then, she turned on some gospel music and we went to sleep with it playing in the background.

The next morning, we had a very nice, warm breakfast with coffee and orange juice. After, we all wrapped up in white robes that were placed in each closet for us and went onto the second-floor balcony. It was cold, but we wanted to take in how beautiful the area was as we looked out to view the mountains, trees, other distant cabins, and our surroundings. Our cabin was so high up all we could see were trees in some areas.

Etta walked to the further right side of the balcony and found the jacuzzi. She stood by as we opened the top to see if it was on and warm; it was. She began to take pictures by the jacuzzi and said, "If it wasn't so cold, I would get in." I thought, *But the water is hot; you'll be fine.* There was also a sitting area in the middle of the balcony on the third floor that we sat in and took more photos, and shared a few more laughs. Kaisha, Mama, and I sat in a chair together with mom in the middle while my aunt took our picture. We were cutting up as usual and laughing about something, so my aunt recorded that moment for us. She started counting down from three to take a picture, but we were still laughing. Mama laughed and said, "Wait a minute, wait a minute. OK come on now, y'all!" As if she wasn't acting up with us. It was a beautiful moment amongst us. After the photos, we went back inside to get ready for our day.

Before the afternoon approached, we set out to explore the town and sightsee. We went to a waterfall trail hike, Fall Branch Falls. I found it online when I was planning things to do on the trip. It was roughly a three-mile, thirty-minute hike from beginning to end, with a beautiful seventy foot drop waterfall. Mama was more excited about it than I thought she would be and even beat me to the top. As we were hiking up, she was a little tired but smiling through it anyway, and she made a few stops at the rest points until we all caught up. I don't think she had ever hiked before. At one of the rest stops, she was sitting with my sister and brother's partner and said, "We tired, but we gone do this thing!" Someone was recording, so then she looked into the camera and said, "What's uuuup," and blew a kiss. She was having a great time in those moments, with not one look over her shoulder. That gave me peace to know that she was safe and able to let go for a while and enjoy herself.

We could hear the waterfall the closer we got to the top. It was beautiful. We took many individual and group pictures together for memories of us. The time spent at the waterfall was needed for us all. After about an hour, we began trailing down and made it back to the van all in one tired piece. Before returning to the cabin, we explored the town a little more, rested our feet, and cleaned up. When we got back, we prepared for a steak dinner on the balcony in our purple pajamas. We had all purchased the same color pj's and slippers online for this night together. We had a great night. It started with food, music, dancing, laughter, and wine. After eating, we went down to the basement to play pool and other games with drinks we had set up for the night. Mama was in the basement first. As I walked down the stairs making a video, she smiled and danced by herself to the music, enjoying that moment alone.

On the fourth day, we had to head home after breakfast. Although the entire trip didn't go as planned, I enjoyed the memories we made and the time spent with each of them. If only it had lasted a little longer.

After safely making it back home, settling in, and discussing our trip with Dad and others, he asked if I would put together a trip in July for the whole family. We hadn't done this in a while. It would be the first time in so long we did anything as a family, with everyone. After taking time and doing some research, I made the plans and rented an Airbnb in Jacksonville, Florida, to visit the zoo and other fun attractions we could enjoy as a family with the kids. Mama came on the trip alone. She taught me how to play a card game called Pitty Pat as we all sat around a big table having a great time and talking mess to one another. It was nice to have the entire family under one big roof. We enjoyed every minute of it. It was the best time we'd had in a while together, without having to worry about something or someone ruining the night. It was needed.

From then on, we continued to get together as often as possible to share moments and memories and enjoy time with one another. We would cook, grill, play cards, laugh, make good fun of each other as families do, and planned to go on more trips. Even if it was just sitting on the front porch together, we made it a thing worthy of memories.

Etta was our hype woman too. When we danced around, she was always in the background hollering and laughing for us to keep going. One evening, a few of us were all sitting on her porch while Sterlyng taught us a dance, as he put it. While dancing, Mama laughed saying, "That's it, do it, that's it!" He kept dancing, and she said, "Ooh, what what—do it!" He kept dancing, and she kept hyping him up.

In August, Tommy decided to run for Homecoming Princess at her school. Mama called to tell me all about it. "You know you have to buy her some clothes and shoes, and get her hair done!" I told her that I would be in town, I'd make sure that everything was taken care of, and that she didn't have to worry about it. I was excited to see my baby competing with the other girls and watching her promo videos. I walked with her onto the field. We wore pink and white. Mama and Kaisha also came to show their support. She brought flowers with her to give to Tommy. She didn't win Homecoming Princess, but we were all still so proud.

Things were pretty quiet, but as October approached, there was this weird energy. Etta seemed nervous or on edge about something. She was different. You could sense that something was going on, but she wouldn't say what. She began calling more throughout the day and sat with my siblings at their houses more. Mama didn't go home until late in the evening some nights. It was like she'd rather stay away from home. We were used to her calls, but something was off in her voice, and we didn't know what. Her voice sounded airy. We were a bit concerned about if there had been any physical violence at home, but she assured us that there was none to worry about. That I believed, because I knew if there were any, she would not stand for it.

One night, Mama, David, and I were sitting in the living room discussing things. David was drinking and watching TV when he began making comments and stating opinions about my siblings that offended me. I mostly brushed them off, because I wasn't surprised this was happening. I was used to this. He would say things to belittle them and compare their lives to others as if he had the right to judge.

I did not want to hear it anymore, so I let him know that I did not appreciate the slander of my siblings, and that maybe he should discuss things with them instead. He became frustrated with me because I tried to put a stop to it. David called me a "firecracker" because I didn't allow him to speak to me disrespectfully or in any way I felt was wrong, and he didn't like it. He said that

I was feisty and thought I ran things, but clearly I didn't. He was just upset because he couldn't treat me the way he treated others.

Standing up to him only seemed to grind his gears more, but I was tired of it. We were going back and forth when my brother walked over from his house. He asked what was going on, so I told him that I was not OK with the way David was speaking of him and our sister. Sterlyng asked him if he really felt that way about them, but of course David denied saying any of the things he had said to Mom and me. He said I was lying. He even tried to bring Mama in the middle by asking her if I was lying. She ignored him because she didn't want to lie and upset my brother, but he knew I was telling the truth.

David and Sterlyng talked things over, smoothly at first. I don't know what was said, but they started yelling, and it turned into a pretty bad argument. I told my brother to go outside to cool off. Then, my sister walked over to Mama's house as I was trying to calm Sterlyng down across the street in his yard. As Kaisha was standing in front of Mama's house facing the front door, she saw David go into the bedroom. The main front door was left open. When he came out of the bedroom, she saw that he had his gun in his hand. He walked into the kitchen, then into the living room, and placed the gun into the holster on his hip. She yelled to us about what she had seen as Mama was standing outside in her yard now too.

In that moment, we were mentally and physically prepared for "war" if it came to it. I was like, *OK, this is it. This is the night I have been dreaming about.* My survival instincts quickly kicked in.

David came outside, and the argument continued as we held my brother back and told him to calm down. But by then, they were going back and forth calling each other names and saying things they would do to each other. Mom was seriously upset. She was silent. Her face looked defeated. She was tired. Etta decided to call one of David's family members to come and pick him up so that he could leave and then maybe things would calm down.

When the family member arrived to pick David up, Mama spoke with him for a while and explained what was going on. She told him she wanted David to leave. That he had been drinking and got upset because he said that I was lying on him about things he had been saying about her children and she's tired of it.

He asked David to come with him, but David said he was not leaving, and the situation didn't get any better. The police were called. When they arrived, Mom informed them of the altercation and said that she wanted him to leave. They told him to put his weapon away, go inside the house alone as they watched, and get all the things he could carry and needed at that time. They told him that he could only return with a police escort for the rest of his belongings, but did he care? No.

After grabbing what he needed, he walked out of the front door and onto the porch with the officers. Etta told him that she wanted her house key. Her voice trembled. In this moment, it seemed like she felt this was her out. That while the police were there, she would be safe to end this relationship and he wouldn't do anything. He was calm while the police were there. Mama was scared. She didn't know what was going to happen that night, but she chose herself, her sanity, and her children's lives, which were threatened multiple times.

He replied, "Are you serious?"

"Yes!" she said.

"This is ridiculous," he said, taking the key off his keyring and giving it to her. Once he left, the police followed to make sure he was gone. After the police were out of sight, he waited about ten minutes before circling back around twice while we were all still outside talking. Then, he decided to stop and get out of his vehicle. He stood in front of his car door and began fussing again, but this time he and Sterlyng were nose to nose.

Sterlyng stood tall and yelled, "I'll do whatever I have to do to protect my mama and my sisters!" Sterlyng had had enough. And no, it wasn't just about that night; it was everything leading up to it too. Emotions were very high.

The police came to Mama's house again, as they had circled backed around, but David made sure to leave because he was told not to come back.

Three weeks later on Saturday, November fifth, Etta's niece had a gathering at her home for her birthday and invited a few of us over to celebrate. Mom, my sister's then-partner, my brother, and I all went over together. The men were outside and the women inside, having good talks, laughs, and carrying on with one another as we do.

Mama's phone rang multiple times. We all saw she was ignoring it on purpose. After a few ignored calls, she said it was her ex calling and she didn't want to talk with him. She ignored it, so we ignored it, and continued our night as planned. Thirty minutes later, Sterlyng came inside upset and told us that David was parked outside at a stop sign across the street from the house, watching and waiting in his car. This made us uncomfortable. We took a few minutes to talk about it, and then went outside to join the others and try to enjoy the rest of the night together. Outside, we saw that he was still sitting in his car at the stop sign across the street. It was dark out with no streetlights in the area where he was parked, but we could still see his car in the light shining from the house.

He was just sitting there, watching.

A few more minutes went by before my sister's partner went across the street to have a conversation with David. To let him know how we were feeling and that he should leave, but he didn't. I texted my sister's partner to come back across the street, because David wasn't bothering anyone. He replied, "Yes, but he aggie as fuck!" But he left David sitting in the car and came back.

Mama watched nervously but still interacted with us. We tried to ignore him, but it was so uncomfortable to be watched like this and not know what he was thinking. My cousin decided to call the police to make him leave. Soon after the police were called, but before they arrived, he left, which was crazy because it was as if he had been informed. There was no way he knew they were called. We questioned if maybe Mama had told him so he would leave right away. When the police got there, they said they would circle back around and make sure David didn't come back, but he didn't.

Around this time, I began to feel a very heavy emotional wave come over me, and all I could do was cry out as others gathered around and asked what was wrong. They talked to me to try and calm me down, but it did not help. I was so overwhelmed and went into a panic. I called my aunt so that I could talk with her about how I was feeling and to make sense of it all. She was the only person I felt like talking to in that moment. I felt out of body. It felt as if I had no control of myself. I don't know what came over me, but it wasn't right.

As I was on the phone with my aunt crying, Mom walked over to me. She asked what was wrong and to whom I was speaking. At first, I couldn't say anything, then suddenly, my emotions took over again. I cried more and begged, "Mama, please stop talking to him. You got to stop. Please, Mama, please leave him alone!" She didn't say anything but instead began crying. Silently, she walked away, and left the party.

Moments later, Dad called and said that Mama was at Kaisha's house crying and upset, saying that she thought I was mad and wouldn't talk with her. He suggested that I call her. But I wasn't mad at Mama. I was just overwhelmed and frustrated with my emotions, and in that moment, what I said and how I said it was the only way I could express them. I don't know why I broke like that.

I spent some time alone before going back to Mama's house. She had made it in before me. Things were extremely quiet in the house as I was getting ready for bed. Mama and I didn't speak for the first hour or so. When I lay down, she came into the room holding up an empty perfume sample bottle that I had once given her to try. She shook the bottle and asked if I would get her another because she liked it and was running out. It felt a little strange, like that night hadn't happened at all, and I wanted to talk to her about it, but it just didn't come out. And she didn't mention anything either. I said, "OK," took the perfume bottle, placed it into my purse, and went to bed.

That was the last I remember of that night; I was exhausted. When I woke up the next day, Mama had already left for work. I stayed at her house for a few hours, packed my things, and then left for home. Occasionally when I visited, I stopped at the nursing home on my way out, but I didn't this time. She texted that night before bed and told me she loved me.

We spoke on the phone a day later. I waited to see if she wanted to talk over everything, but she didn't bring it up. Instead, we talked about my move to Fort Campbell, and I asked if she could be at my house with me when the movers arrive. I also asked about the kids. I was emotional and still needed time to process what I was feeling. I couldn't shake this feeling that something was wrong or was going to happen. Something bad.

November ninth was a rest day for Etta. She usually relaxed and cleaned around the house but had a few things to take care of that morning. I called to ask if she could go to my daughter's school to sign a withdrawal form, because we were relocating within the next thirty days. She replied that she would do so after getting an oil change for her car at Terwilliger. She said she would be sitting at my sister's job as she waited.

Throughout the day, I felt the need to call and talk with Mama about anything I could think of, no matter how small it was. I didn't want to end any of our calls and felt frustrated every time she said she needed to call back. I would wait a while, then pick the phone back up to call her again if I hadn't heard from her. I couldn't explain what I was feeling, but I knew it wasn't normal. I needed Mama's presence, but I was back home and had appointments that day, so the phone was the best option.

Later that afternoon while on three-way call with my siblings, they said David went over to see Mama but weren't sure why. We took a few minutes to talk and expressed our thoughts and feelings about it before hanging up. Sterlyng said this had been going on long enough. He also felt that he must protect Mama. Kaisha was mainly quiet and listened as we spoke. I told them that there was nothing we could do, because she had to be the one to put a stop to things. I was upset, but it was true and needed to be said.

Afterward, I called Mama again to check in and ask if she had gone to sign the withdrawal form. Honestly, I was calling to make sure she was not with David. I must have called at least five times that day to talk and remind her of the form, but she was mostly quiet and listened. I probably was on her nerves by that point. She said it had slipped her mind, but she would go before school ended and would call back later because she was talking with my uncle as he did something in the yard.

Around three in the afternoon, Mama called while in the school's office to make sure she filled the form out correctly and asked if I needed a copy. She also said she was going to take Tommy home with her, but Tommy was already on the bus. I told her to keep a copy of the form for me and that it was OK. We ended the call.

As Tommy walked home after getting off the school bus, she called me. She said as she was walking home from the bus stop, one of her friends told her that David was coming up the road in his car from behind them. He drove up beside her slowly as she walked and asked her questions, but she chose not to talk with him. I told her that it was OK if she did not want to talk and to go inside the house, lock all the doors, and wait for Mom to return home.

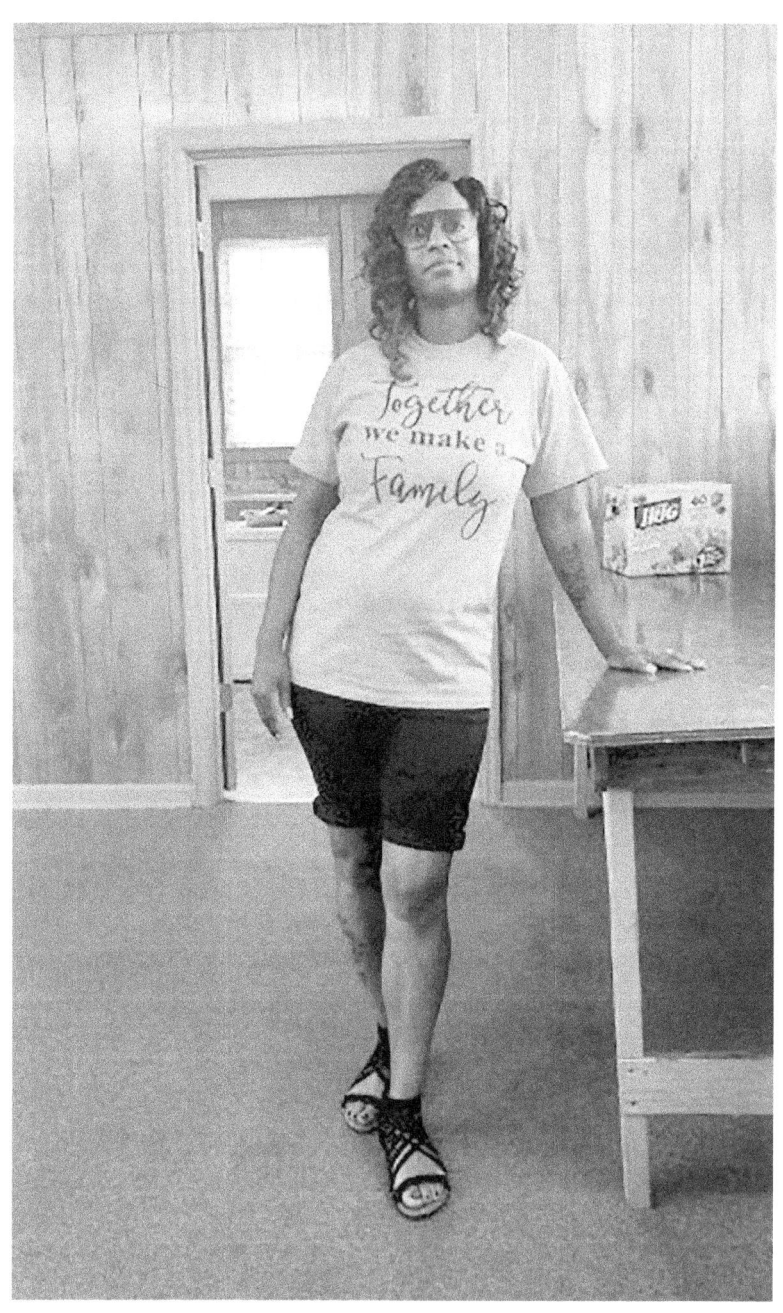

Mama at a family function

A November to Remember

I would lay in bed most mornings with my eyes open, staring up at the ceiling, watching the fan spin slowly, talking and praying to God. I asked for understanding of the things I was seeing and feeling and of the fear I was feeling. I spoke over the things that were troubling my mind and spirit. The nightmares were a burden, and I needed them to stop.

The more I prayed, the clearer they became. This was a warning. I should have known what they were from other times God had allowed me to see and know things, but I was in denial.

Although it had been three weeks since Etta ended her relationship, she often communicated with her ex. As her children, we were proud of her for making the best decision for her. It also felt like it was for us, and as a mother myself, I know what that feels like. We tried our best to keep things as normal as possible during this new change in her life, to keep her mind off recent troubles or wondering as much as we could.

Mama didn't open up much about what she was feeling and going through mentally or emotionally. But we noticed she seemed nervous. Sometimes she would fidget, cautiously looking around as she spoke, and occasionally looking over her shoulders as if she was being watched or followed. But she kept quiet.

November ninth was an early day. I took my son to school that morning and ran errands while Mama and I shared a few calls and texts that continued into the afternoon. Kaisha and Sterlyng were both working, but Sterlyng suddenly felt ill and went home by that afternoon. He had been trying to reach Mama throughout the day but couldn't get through to her. Someone reached out and told him that David was sitting in his car alone in a nearby area, up the street from their house. Sitting, watching, and waiting— maybe waiting for her to come home. When Sterlyng arrived home, Mama's car was not out front where she normally parked. He called her again, but still, no answer.

Later in the evening, Etta spent some time at Sterlyng's house while getting her hair done, and he described the physical exhaustion that had come over his body. He felt weak, had no appetite, couldn't keep his eyes open, and said that he felt as if his body was shutting down, but couldn't explain why. He went to bed early while Mama's hair was being finished.

At 8:51 p.m., Tommy informed me that Mama was going to take David something she cooked, because he'd asked her to. Kaisha, her children, and Tommy all went with her to take him the food. At 8:58 p.m., Tommy texted that after Mom finished talking with him, he told them he loved them and apologized. He was standing outside of the car and reeked of alcohol. I told her that she did not have to interact if she was uncomfortable. At 9:04 p.m., she texted that they were headed to my sister's house for a while, and shortly after, I went to bed.

At 11:41 p.m., she texted again, *Ma, he over here.* Then again, *We pulled up and he was over here.* At 11:53 p.m., she texted, *Maaa!*

but I was still sleeping. I did not see the messages when she sent them.

My phone rang at 11:59 p.m. It was Tommy. She sounded agitated as she explained to me that when they were pulling into the yard at home to park, David was already there, sitting on the porch. He was waiting for Mama to get home and seemed to be on foot, as his car was nowhere in sight. They were still outside when Tommy called. She told me he had asked Mama to take him to his car, but she said no. Then he asked if he could use the bathroom. Mom told him yes, but he would have to leave right after.

As they went into the house, I was still on the phone and could hear talking in the background. I told Tommy to place the phone close by her bedroom door, so that I could hear what David and Mama were talking about. I wanted to hear everything being said. She said that they were standing near the outside of her bedroom door. By this time, I was worried, because I was aware that he had already been drinking earlier that night and was intoxicated.

She placed the phone near her door and I listened. I heard him ask Mama if he could stay, but she told him no and to leave. I called Tommy's name to pick the phone back up, but she didn't hear me the first few times. Once she picked up the phone, she informed me that she had walked away to the kitchen. I could still hear them talking in the background.

The conversation between David and Etta was not an argument; he was just begging to come back home to stay. I asked Tommy to place the phone back by the door again, so she did.

He continued to ask if he could stay the night, but Mama kept her word, said no, and encouraged him to get some help. He said it had been three weeks already and that he was tired of sleeping on his nephew's couch. He then asked her, "You just going to let thirteen years go to waste like that?"

I could still clearly hear her begging him to leave, but he wouldn't go, so eventually, I called Tommy's name again. When she picked up, I asked her to put Mama on the phone. Once I was on the phone with Mama, I asked if she needed me to call anyone, but she said no. I asked her if she needed me to have someone come and take Tommy away, but again, she said, "No, he's going to leave." She assured me. I didn't want Tommy around if he was going to end up staying over that night in his condition, so I made her aware of how I felt.

In the background, I could hear him asking Mama, "Who are you talking to?" She ignored him.

I said, "Ok, will you give her the phone back?"

I was a little upset, because Mom didn't want any help from me, and I wasn't there in case something did happen. When Tommy was back on the phone, I told her to put it back by the door so I could continue to listen. Part of this was also me just being nosey about what was happening and being said. Again, it was not an argument—no voices were raised and it sounded under control.

He asked again, "Can I stay?" And then, "Who was on the phone?"

Mama sounded annoyed, and she replied firmly, "No, and don't worry about it!"

He then asked, "Is the police coming?" She said no and still didn't tell him that it was me on the phone. She kind of just let him wonder.

He went back to asking if he could stay, and she replied, "No, and I'm not going to keep being nice about it!" At this point I sat up in bed, because I was alarmed by her response to him and didn't know how he'd react.

Their conversation continued with no yelling or arguing, just repeated questions and repeated answers by both of them. Like a broken record. He was not accepting no for an answer.

Then, everything went silent for a few seconds. The phone was still by the door. I called my daughter's name to ask what was happening, but she couldn't hear me. When she did pick up the phone, she said that he had stepped to her bedroom door, looked her in the face, and closed her door slowly. It made her uncomfortable.

We continued to talk, and I was listening as hard as I could to the background, because at this point, it was a little muffled. I heard him ask if he could stay again, Mama said, "No, and I'm not saying it again!"

I heard him say, "I got something for—" I couldn't make out if it was "this" or "that."

Next, I heard Mama call out his name in a panic, scared, and fearful tone. Then she yelled, "No!" I thought he was getting physical with her. I couldn't hear anything from him, though; he was silent as far as I could tell, but I could hear Mom loud and clear. I got very emotional and scared. I sat up even more in bed. Mama began screaming and yelling at the top of her lungs saying, "David you don't have to do this!" She begged him.

Gunshots fired.

From what I could make out through the phone, it sounded as if Mom had run through the front door and outside to try and get away from him. I heard her horrible screams as the shots continued but sounded further away. Then suddenly, she stopped, I couldn't hear her anymore. *What is happening? Why can't I hear Mama?* I thought frantically.

When the shots first fired, my daughter screamed. I asked her what was going on as she was screaming and crying, "Mama, he shooting, he's shooting at Nana!" I began crying and my mind was in a million places deciding what to tell her to do next. I stood up and cried, "Hide, get under the bed, or run!" I was panicking. She cried, "Mama, I can't; I'm scared!" I could still hear shots as we both cried. I screamed, "Run and call 911!"

She cried and screamed as the shots got louder, and then the call dropped. My heart dropped too.

Please God, not my baby girl!

It seemed that my heart immediately fell to the floor, because in that moment, I knew that not only might I lose my mother but my baby girl too. To me, the only explanation for the shots getting louder was that he had come back into the house after my daughter. I tried multiple times to call her back but there was no answer, it went straight to voicemail with each call. I immediately began to question and blame myself. Did I trigger him with the phone call because he thought I was the police? Should I have had my daughter call the police from the beginning, even though Mama said she was OK? If I did, then maybe this would not have happened. Why didn't I listen to my gut feeling and do it anyway? What did I do? This is all my fault! This is all my fault.

Chapter 9

"The Long Road Home"

I screamed at the top of my lungs while pacing and running back and forth around the house in shock. My mind couldn't catch up to what was happening to me. *What can I do, Lord?* I went back into my bedroom and put on the first clothes I could reach. I ran into the living room and my knees went weak; I dropped to the floor between the front door and couch and screamed as loud as I could. I tried getting up, but my knees were so weak, numb. I dropped into the fetal position on my elbows and knees, pressed my forehead against the floor between my elbows and let out the loudest scream I could again.

After almost falling over, I calmed down a bit and called 911 at 12:30 a.m. before going to the car. A female dispatcher answered, and I was screaming and crying trying to talk to her. She asked me to calm down so she could understand me clearly. I took a deep breath, calmed myself, and told her what was going on and where. She informed me that she would have to give me the number to the Swainsboro police department because it was out of our district.

I was frustrated because I felt that she could have done more to help, but she gave me the number and told me that she would call back to check if I had gotten ahold of anyone. My frustration wasn't really with her, and I did understand she did what she could in that moment, but I was confused and in shock.

At 12:33 a.m., I called my sister and told her what had happened; then Dad, and then I tried my baby girl again, but still no answer. At 12:34 a.m. I called my cousin that lived not too far from Mama. Then I dialed the number to the police department, but no one answered. The time didn't occur to me until the phone kept ringing, and I realized the dispatch had given me the number to the police department's front desk. They were closed.

Once I was able to regain my strength, I went into my son's room, wrapped him with a blanket, went into the garage, and placed him into the car. I went back into the house to grab my phone.

I called a close friend, screaming and crying again. He asked, "What's going on Domanique?" but I couldn't speak at first. I gathered myself and told him some of what had happened. He asked if I needed him to pick me up, but I said no because I was already leaving and was not going to wait. I quickly hung up the phone and got into the car. I drove as fast as I could with the emergency lights on. I called my son's dad and explained that I needed to take our son to a family member's house once I got in town, because I did not want to take him with me to Mama's.

I was crying on the phone when my son woke up and overheard me telling his dad what had happened. He cried out, "He shot Nana! I want my Nana!" I calmed him down as best I could; I felt bad that he heard me, because I didn't want him to know what happened.

Next I called my first sergeant and commander but didn't get an answer, so I called the lieutenant. I told him everything while crying. He was sad for me and said that he would send the information to proper personnel. He asked some questions my unit would need answers to and said that he would call back if more information was needed.

Dad called and asked for my location. I told him that I was already on the way there. He said he did not want me driving in the state of mind I was in and that he would meet me and have someone come with him to drive for me. I said OK and hung up. I called my brother to ask what was going on and if my baby girl was OK. He stated that she was with the police and her aunt giving her statement of the incident. I asked him about Mom even though deep down I already knew, I could feel it. He sadly replied, "She's gone Domanique!" I began crying again.

After Sterlyng and I finished talking, the female dispatcher called back and asked if I had gotten any help. I told her my daughter was OK and that she was with the police. Before hanging up, I thanked her for trying to help and calling back to check on us. I wasn't expecting her call back at all.

As I was coming upon exit 104, Dad called again to let me know his whereabouts. He told me to pull over because he was close. I was upset because I didn't want to stop driving. I felt that I would lose time and I wanted to drive as fast as I could to get there as soon as I could. I turned onto the exit and parked at a store. The lieutenant called back for more information while Dad was pulling in behind me.

When Dad parked, my brother's partner got out of his truck as the phone was still to my ear. I got out of my car while holding on to it for support. I felt weak and sick to my stomach. She asked if I was OK, and I said, "Yes, I'm just weak!" As I got into the passenger side of my car, I finished talking on the phone and hung up. She drove and we discussed what had happened. She told me that she heard the gunshots; they woke her. She then woke my brother and told him that she heard shots. He thought she was just hearing things at first but to be sure, he looked out his bedroom window, saw something beside Mama's car, and immediately recognized Mama's shoes. They quickly ran outside.

She said that she kneeled over Mama and began CPR, but when she checked her pulse, there was none. She could also see that there was a gunshot wound to the head, but she kept going until the ambulance arrived. The EMT took over but couldn't save her. She said that Mama was on her side, kind of balled up into a position of protection. She continued to share her emotions and what she saw as I cried. She was shaken up as well but still focused enough on the drive. Then I received a text with an address so that I could drop my son off before going to Mama's.

As we made our way into town, closer to Mama's house, I asked her to drop me off first, then my son at the address I received. Once we made it to Mom's street, we saw cars everywhere and red and blue lights flashing so brightly. She said that we may not be able to pull all the way up. I told her to stop the car and I would run the rest of the way. She said she'd keep trying, but I told her to stop or I was going to jump out. She pulled over, and I rushed out of the car and ran as fast as I could up the road to get to Mama and my baby girl.

This was all still like a dream to me, not real at the time. But my body was reacting like it was real; my mind was confused and I felt lost. A part of me knew Mama was going to be OK, but the other part also knew she wasn't, and this was real. It was a nightmare I couldn't shake. I needed to wake from it, but it felt so real. As I continued running, the police and ambulance lights grew brighter and brighter. I ran even faster. My feet weren't moving fast enough.

I saw body figures but couldn't make out who they were, because it was dark with only one streetlight ahead. I heard someone shout out "Domanique is here!" I then saw Dad, a female police officer, and yellow tape wrapped around a pole. I went into complete shock, with nothing but getting to Mama on my mind. I felt nothing. I heard nothing. Saw nothing. I looked out behind the ambulance and on the ground next to Mama's car. I saw a body figure under a bright white sheet. I felt rage and ran straight to that sheet that laid ahead.

Dad and the officer quickly grabbed and stopped me before I made it under the yellow tape. I cried, screamed, and yelled, "Get off of me!" Another male police officer came to help as I continued yelling "Let me go, get off of me!... Mama, get up!" Dad yelled for me to calm down, but I wouldn't. I used all my strength and managed to push back enough from all three people holding me back to start running again.

Before I ducked my head under the tape, though, someone grabbed me again. It was my uncle. He pulled me to his chest, held me tight, and said, "It's OK baby, I got you." I immediately felt weak; sadness overcame me, and I fell to the ground. But my uncle held on tightly and went down with me. I cried and screamed in his arms. "They wouldn't let me go. Please, I want to see Mama!"

As I looked back beyond the tape, I watched this body under a sheet lying flat on the stretcher. Still in shock, I asked myself, "Is that really Mommy? Is this really happening?" I could make out the parts of her body: her head, arms, stomach, and legs. I could see that her feet were pointing toward the sky as she lay under this bright white sheet.

I was weak, numb, crying, begging, and waiting for Mama to get up and tell me that everything was going to be alright, but she didn't move.

I wanted to hold her, tell her how much I loved her, and to see for myself that it was really her. I was out of my mind but I knew I needed her. They just wouldn't let me go to her. I became so angry while still on the ground with my uncle. I watched them raise the stretcher, leaving behind a small pool of her blood beside her car where she lay. They pushed her toward the back of the ambulance, where the doors were wide open and red and blue lights still flashed. There was a pause. My uncle helped me up from the ground, and I watched them push the stretcher into the back of the ambulance to drive away. I felt the need to run again and jump in the back and go with her, but I was still in shock, and frozen. My feet felt glued to the ground. I could not move or wake from this terrible nightmare.

At this point, my brain still had not processed that my daughter was, in fact, alive and well. I hadn't seen her yet. All I could see now was a male police officer removing the yellow tape with his right hand and wrapping it loosely around his left.

Standing outside by Mama's car, looking at the blood, anger filled every inch of my body. I could feel it in my toes and fingertips and in my eyes. I yelled for someone to make it disappear. I was so upset that the blood was there, and everyone could see it. "Make it go away!" Sterlyng immediately came over to me and said he'd take care of it. He went to get water and poured it over the blood to wash it away as we cried. While doing so, he was holding on to a rag in his hand. It had fresh red stains on it. Mama's blood, to be exact. He wiped her face when he found her before the police had arrived. It broke him.

I looked at the car on the side where Mama lay, around it and under. Sterlyng asked, "What are you doing?" I told him that I was looking for bullet shells or holes, blood, dents in the car, or anything from the shooting, but I didn't find anything. The police had it all for evidence, of course, even her purse, because it was beside her when they arrived. I don't know exactly why I was searching, but I did.

I made my way into the house and scanned the walls to see if there were any bullet holes there, because the shooting began in the house, but I got nothing. *Why am I doing this to myself?*

I went into Mama's bedroom, laid in her bed, and cried out again. Sterlyng came into the room and sat down beside me as I cried in his arms, and he told me he loved me. I looked across the room and saw Mama's gold watch on the dresser that she wore sometimes; it was Grandma's watch. I rushed to grab it then and quickly realized the battery was dead. I cried and asked, "Why isn't it working? I need this to work!" Sterlyng hugged me and promised to get it working again.

"The battery might be dead," he said. I slid it onto my wrist and cried some more while he stayed by my side.

Others came inside and crowded around. I got up, went into the bathroom, and closed the door. A wave of anger and rage took over at once. I'd never felt anything like that before and wasn't sure what to do with it. I looked around and began to react uncontrollably. I started destroying the bathroom. I threw a few things that were on the sink around and knocked over everything I could. My daughter's dad rushed in, grabbed me, and eased me down to the floor outside of the bathroom door. I heard him ask Tommy to come sit with me, and then he went back into the bathroom to clean up the mess I had made.

As I was sitting on the floor with my back against the washer, I went into a daze with my knees to my chest. Tommy walked over silently, sat on the floor in front of and to the right of me with her back to the wall, and just stared at me. She placed her right hand on my right knee and said, "Mama, I'm OK. I'm right here in front of you." It didn't register for me that this was her. I couldn't feel anything. I couldn't say anything. I was numb. I felt that I had lost everything. My mama, my baby girl, and myself, all at once. She wasn't real to me at that moment, and I couldn't feel her.

After silently sitting for a while, we stood up and she hugged me. Then I slowly walked to the couch and sat down. My body went into shock and started reacting. I was shaking and trembling nonstop from head to toe; my body tightened. My arms were tightly squeezed into my sides, and it hurt. I couldn't control it. Everyone around was asking if I was OK, but I didn't speak or move. I could only blink my eyes. My family was worried. I closed my eyes to see only darkness and try and calm myself. I heard someone say that I should be taken to the hospital for help. That maybe they could do something to calm my body.

A few moments later, there were hands gently lifting me to a car parked in front of the house to go to the hospital. My cousin drove me. When we arrived, she ran inside and came out with a wheelchair and two nurses. I was placed in the wheelchair and rolled inside as the nurses talked to me. They asked questions that I tried to answer, but my mouth wasn't making a sound. I went mute. The nurses pushed me into a room and placed me onto a bed while my mind and body went into a silent panic, because I saw a white sheet. My blood pressure was horrible. My eyes were blurry. *Shake this off Domanique*, I said to myself. *I'm scared!*

Dad and other visitors came to the hospital, and my older cousin and her husband stayed at my bedside. Dad said that my friend was in the waiting room and wanted to see me. I didn't want anyone else in at that time, but I couldn't give the nurses what they needed, so he came in and gave them my information. I overheard the nurse after she spoke with him and realized it was my mother they had just brought in. She immediately came in to offer comfort. She held my hand and explained that she would need to give me something to help my body relax. She walked away and came back a few minutes later to give me a shot and told me to rest. After a few moments had passed, I felt my body slowly, finally calm down and regain some of what I felt to be losing: my mind. My arms released from my sides and my teeth weren't chattering against each other as much.

"Wake up, Domanique. Wake up already!"

After a few hours of trying to relax, I was released from the hospital and taken back to Mama's house. I laid in her bed, wrapped myself in her covers with her pillow in my arms, and stared at the dark. I lay awake wishing I had asked to see her before I left the hospital. Still needing to make sure it was really her.

I felt afraid to fall asleep; I didn't sleep at all. My nerves were shot and my body was aching. I was heartbroken, angry, confused, and now lonely.

Chapter 10

"Absent from the Body and to Be Present with the Lord"

—2 Corinthians 5:8

I realized the sun was coming up and I hadn't slept at all. After a few hours of staring at the walls, I paced the house a bit, went outside, and took another look around while it was light out. Candles, flowers, and a white teddy bear were placed beside Mama's car. I stepped back onto the porch and scanned everything. I found small, splattered blood spots on the beams by my daughter's bedroom window and on the wood of the porch. I instantly went into Mama mode. I did not want anyone to see this. I quickly went inside to grab cleaning supplies and something to help scrape off the blood if needed. I tried to clean the blood but soon realized that some of it had already stained the white paint. With tears in my eyes and questions running through my mind, I scraped as hard as I could to make it disappear. I needed it all gone.

Why can't I just close my eyes, fall asleep, and wake up to this all being a horrible dream?

My eyes are swollen.

My head hurts.

My heart is broken, and my body still aches.

I went back inside and tried to relax my mind and body.

Later that afternoon, my siblings, daughter, and I all gathered to talk over what happened and check in with one another.

Kaisha shared her thoughts from when I called her and said that right after I hung up, she walked to Mama's house from her apartment. Then my daughter shared.

Tommy said that when she and Mama approached the house, a sudden worry overcame her. It looked as if David had been waiting for Mama to get home that night, and because he had already been drinking, she asked Mama to keep driving after she saw him. She asked her not to get out of the car, but Mama told her that everything was going to be OK. She also stated that when the shots got louder, it was because she had walked toward the front door while he was shooting to see what was happening.

She was in shock and couldn't explain why she had chosen to go to the door, but she saw him firing down toward the ground on the other side of the car. She couldn't see Mama at that moment and that's when she hung up the phone with me to call the police. This explained why my calls were going straight to voicemail. She then ran out of the back door, jumped the fence, and ran down the street to where a friend lived. When she looked back up the road, David had already started running away, in the opposite direction from where she was.

Sterlyng had a conversation with a nearby neighbor. He stated that before Mama returned home, he did see David around the house, which seemed off to him, but he didn't say anything and went inside his home. He was unaware of what was going on. Another nearby neighbor also stated that they saw him running past their house.

As he fled the scene, someone called our aunt. She and our uncle drove to the hospital where they thought Mama was taken at the time, because they were unaware that she had not been transported yet. They spotted him. My uncle tried to get out of the car, but my aunt kept driving so that he couldn't get out. She called the police to inform them of David's whereabouts. Soon after, he was taken into custody with his firearm by the police.

Sterlyng also stated that before Mama's return home, David came to his house and was knocking on the door with his weapon in hand. He was not aware of this until they checked the camera footage from that night. He said he felt as if the shooting was meant for him, not Mama, so he felt guilty and like he was to blame.

After a few days had passed. We had our first court appearance and were unaware if David would be present or not. Emotions were high, but we had to show up for Mama the best we could. We spoke with our attorney before heading into the courtroom, and she informed us that David would, in fact, be present. It got quiet and my heart was beating fast as we all looked around the room at one another. I checked to make sure Tommy was OK, and she said, "I'm OK. I have to do this for Nana!"

We also spoke briefly with Sterlyng to make sure he would be OK. He said he was, but he wasn't. He spoke out—loudly—on a few things he was feeling. It caught the attention of the attorney, judge, and others, so instead of bringing David into the courtroom, they placed him into a separate room and showed him on a screen as the judge went over his charges and read the coroner's report. He stated the charges were of multiple counts and that Mama was wounded six times.

Chapman Funeral Home of Swainsboro was chosen to officiate the funeral. Their employees were so kind and patient with us. They helped and carried us through the entire process, from beginning to end, and even some time after their services were no longer needed. My siblings and I picked out a beautiful all-white casket with gold chrome trim, flowers, and her outfit, which was royal blue and white, two of her favorite colors. She also loved the color red.

On November fourteenth I was happy to have the opportunity to spend a few hours alone with Mama at the funeral home before the viewing and to help with the last few touches needed for her. I was nervous. I had packed a few things in a bag: products to do her hair and makeup, her favorite perfume, and pearl bracelets that my sister and I purchased. My family was shocked that I had agreed to do this, but I needed to. I'd rather it was me. I told them that I was OK, then left Mama's house.

Once I arrived at the funeral home and parked, I sat in my car a moment and prayed.

"God, please strengthen and guide me. Help me to do this one last thing for Mama, my best friend. With no interruptions, no feelings of guilt or blame, and no brokenness, just me and my love for her. God, please be my strength and allow me to do what needs to be done for not only me but for Mama as well. Thank you for allowing me this last moment with her, and for granting me with being able to say my final goodbye. In your name I pray, Amen!"

As I entered, I was greeted with care, sympathy, and a gentle hug. I spoke for a moment with the employees; they seemed happy to have me and acknowledged my strength for what I was about to do, because not many could do it. They guided me down the hall until we reached double doors. I was asked if I needed anything and if I would like someone to stay with me throughout my time with her for support. I asked to be alone and requested that they just check in with me from time to time to be sure. They assured me they would, and then we entered the viewing room.

Mama was lying flat on her back on a table in the middle of the room. There was a sheet covering from her stomach down. I asked about all her wounds and the exact places they were, so I knew before getting started. I wasn't sure if I asked because I needed to know to be aware and prepared in case I saw them, or if I just wanted to know exactly where they were. An employee informed me of the wound locations, gave me a bottle of water, and exited the room.

Mama's dress and coverup were already placed on her. I adjusted them the way I needed them to be. I scanned her face. She had scars on her left side from her temple down to her cheek, as if she had scraped the ground when she fell. I rubbed her cheek and told her "I'm here" and how much I loved her.

I connected my phone to a Bluetooth speaker in the room for music.

As I rubbed her hair, I stared at the wound on her left temple. I had to cover it. I decided to place a wig on her that I had packed to hide the scar so others wouldn't see. Since she had just gotten her hair done, I had to take some of it out to place the wig on properly. I placed more makeup to hide the scrapes down the side of her face, applied natural lipstick to her lips, and put eyeliner and mascara on. I wanted to be a part of every piece of her last and final appearance, which she took so much pride in. I had to make her proud. This felt right. It's what I needed.

I don't know how many times I kissed and rubbed her chilled forehead in those three short hours. I talked and laughed with her. I could feel her presence and hear her voice in the room with me. I heard her laugh and saw her beautiful smile on her face. I could hear her singing with me as her favorite gospel songs played while I held her hand. We gossiped a little about my siblings and her grandchildren. I needed her to know that even though I was her baby girl, I had this family now and she could rest.

She was so beautiful and at peace.

My body was physically present, but my mind was still unaware of reality and what was happening. It's hard to explain—I was numb to everything happening in those moments with her. There was no anger or sadness but a sense of peace for me. And not just for me, but for her, because she was now finally free. I believe that is the reason I was able to do as I did for her in those final hours. I knew she was happy now. There was not one tear dropped. It was the most beautiful, calming, reassuring, and necessary time. It felt passionate. I could even smell her. In those moments, she allowed me to know that she was OK, would never leave my side, and that this was not the end of her story.

Before I was done taking every advantage of our time together, I sprayed her favorite perfume on us both and exited the room. The director and staff were waiting patiently outside of the viewing room and asked me to wait a few minutes as they went in and placed her into the casket. After, I reentered the room and went to her; they had pushed the casket to the wall across the room from the double doors. I was happy that her wounded side faced the inside of the casket and wall. I adjusted her clothing and hair, placed the bracelets onto her wrist, and kissed her forehead once more. While I was doing those things, the director came back into the room with her name sticker and asked if I would like to help place it on the bottom of the casket; I did. It was embroidered with gold writing.

Once we were done, they told me it was time I go home to get ready for the viewing, which was in about forty-five minutes. I walked out of the room while looking back at Mama, not wanting to leave. I spoke with the director and others once more and then went back to Mama's house to join the rest of the family in getting ready for the viewing.

As we all entered the funeral home, we were greeted by the employees and the sign I requested that said no phones for pictures. Everyone lined up at the closed double doors. Once the doors opened, we saw a screen playing her favorite gospel song, "Let It Rain" by Bishop Paul Morton, with a lot of photos of Mama and us on screen. I had already taken my well-needed time with Mama so for the most part I was OK. Of course, there was crying and sadness from us all, but Dad was especially not OK.

He was at Mama's casket the entire time, crying and saying that he was not leaving her or from her side no matter what. Dad wasn't having it. He said he was not moving, and he didn't. I tried to get his sister and girlfriend to talk to him, but they couldn't get him to back down either. I told them that it was OK, to let him be and we would watch over him. He stood at Mama's head, kissed her, wrapped his left arm around the top of her head, and cried like I've never seen him cry before. We had never seen Dad like this, and it hurt my siblings and me to see it. He cried when his brother passed, but this was different. He said she was the love of his life and he wished she would have just come home to him, and this wouldn't have happened. He was completely heartbroken.

This was the love I always knew, the love I want one day, and the love we all crave. Though this was a difficult time, to witness this made my heart a little less heavy, because I've always been in awe of my daddy's love. It was an amazing, faithful, and loyal kind of love that never wavered, even in death.

Before leaving, my daughter, sister, and I all took a bracelet from Mama's wrist and placed them on ours for keeps.

How could someone do this to a woman like Etta? She was such an amazing person to everyone and tried to make everyone happy and feel loved, appreciated, and cared for. She gave her last. Food from her table, clothes from her closet, shoes off her feet, and a place to stay when needed. She didn't deserve any of this, no one does. Although not everyone was accepting of the love and kindness she offered, she did it without complaining, even if it wasn't returned. This was wrong. She did not deserve this.

The funeral was the next day on November fifteenth at Swainsboro Auditorium, and the burial was in a small country town where our grandmother rests. We all wore blue, white, and black with blue ribbons that were gifted to us by a close friend. It was crowded outside of Mama's house before the drive to the Auditorium. I held my head down. We prayed as a family and were escorted to the limos, where it suddenly hit me what I had done. I had planned my mother's funeral and I was not ready for this. A wave of sadness came over me and all I could do was cry and ask, "What have I done? I'm not ready; I need more time!" My family assured me that it was OK and that I had done so well thus far, but I didn't care to hear that. I was so hurt and heartbroken that this day had come and felt that more time might help me feel better.

As the hearse and limos parked and they rolled out the casket for the entrance, I felt sick. The doors of our limo opened. We were slowly escorted into the Auditorium, following inches behind the casket. My knees were weak and I could barely keep my eyes open. I froze. There was this long walk ahead. My cousin rushed to my side, walked with me, and sat beside me. We were escorted inside to view Mom and then to our seats. Others walked in behind us and viewed her as well. They greeted us, shook our hands, hugged our necks, and briefly gave their respects before going to their seats.

After everyone was seated, the funeral director and staff employees gathered around from every angle, as it was time to close the casket while soft music played. My stomach turned and I dropped my head, because I did not want to see this happening, but there was a hand reaching out to me. As I slowly looked up, I saw it was the director. He asked if I would like to do the honors of saying my last goodbye and closing the casket for the very last time.

I took a deep breath, placed my left hand in his, and let him and my cousin help me up slowly. I was escorted to the head of Mama's right side. *She's resting and at peace*, I said in my head. I felt her presence again. I scanned her once more, adjusted her top clothing again, rubbed from her forehead down her left and right cheeks with the back of my right hand, and briefly held her right hand. I fixed her hair, kissed her forehead, whispered once more in her ear that I loved her, and said my final goodbye.

It was time to close the casket.

My heart pounded loudly.

I was guided to tuck in the sides of the casket liner, then slowly begin closing, but before it was completed, I froze again. I used the little strength I had left to stop the closing. I needed a moment to wrap my head around this. Suddenly, a hand was gently placed over my right hand to help guide me in the completion of closing and locking the casket.

I went numb.

The program was beautiful and very intimate. Mama's co-workers from the nursing home had so many good memories to share. They presented us with a signed uniform top from everyone she worked with that was framed nicely. Everyone that spoke gave us all a little bit more of her to laugh at, appreciate, and hold on to.

When the program came to an end, everyone began exiting the Auditorium with flowers; the drive to the site was near. It was a bit of a drive, which felt like it took days, but I was ok with this part dragging out. We were not fully ready for this last and final bye, but it had to be done now; we had to face this together as a family.

After sitting in my seat at the site, I went into a daze and drowned everything out with my thoughts. I wondered what life would have been like if we were still a family with Dad, living together and traveling. Maybe we would have another house dog. Mama had one named Snoopy when we were younger, a gift to her from Dad. Snoopy had a lot of energy, but he got out one day on his own, went onto the road, and was hit by a car. Mama was so hurt, and Dad tried to get her another, but she didn't want one.

Maybe we would still be traveling in dad's Lincoln with Mama on the passenger side as I talked the entire trip. Mama would look out the car window up into the dark sky at the beautiful moon and stars, deep in thought. Sterlyng and Kaisha would be sound asleep with smiles on their faces and heads leaning on the cold windows.

Maybe we could have been just a simple family that enjoyed being home together. Mama cooking Sunday meals before Dad's work week began. We would visit the corner store where the owner grilled burgers for us often. Then, she would push us gently on the swings at the park across the road as we laughed with enjoyment.

Before the lowering of the casket, everyone was expected to leave, but a few of us stayed behind for a moment. Once we began to walk toward the limo, everything went dark. I collapsed to the ground, let out the loudest cry, and screamed as loudly as I could. I couldn't control my body or feel anything, not even my legs and arms. I felt like a little girl again, but lost and motherless. Family members rushed over to help me from the ground, and others shouted to leave me be because this was my moment. I had held it in long enough. The rest gave me the space and time to finally let it all out. I had been trying to hold it all together and did so well that I robbed myself by not allowing myself to feel the grief and pain.

It hurt.

After I gathered myself enough to feel my legs again, the director and driver supported me as I got back into the limo. We drove to the repast, but while I was there, I felt so alone that I needed to leave. I didn't want to be around anyone at all. Dad's partner took me back to Mama's where I crawled in her bed, balled up with her pillows, and cried in silence, with no one there but me and my sadness.

I needed Mama, but she was gone.

Journal Entry

I wish I could say that I am OK but, truthfully, I'm not. My heart is broken. My body is numb. I feel detached from everything and everyone. I feel nothing. My eyes are hurting. I only see darkness and I'm scared of the dark. There is emptiness in my heart and it's hard to trust anyone or let them in right now. I don't quite understand what I am feeling just yet or how to express it, but I know that I am lost.

There's this dark corner in my room where I see the little girl I used to be. She's around five or six years old. She sits and cries with her knees to her chest and arms wrapped tightly around them. She places her head on her knees while asking for Mama, but I don't have an answer for her. I hate that she's hurting like this; it's not fair. It feels as if our souls have been separated and I don't know how to reconnect with her right now. As I leave her there, she becomes angry. I must find my way back to her, because I need her as much as she needs me.

I haven't had many good days. They all feel painful. I feel guilty if I crack a smile or laugh at something. Why can't I move on like everyone else around me? My thoughts are not always clear nor pure. My emotions are not aligned, anger is knocking to become my friend, and hate tries to creep in, but it won't take control of me. I need to scream and shout, kick, and hit something or someone. I know I need therapy, but being that I refuse to accept this, wouldn't it be pointless? A waste of their time? Denial. I need someone to talk to about this before I lose my mind.

I lie awake at night with the TV on for light until the morning comes. I'm traumatized. I check all the locks in my home every hour. I don't know why I feel so unsafe. I'm tired. I feel myself drowning, and though I can swim I'm not sure if I even want to come up for air. It feels like I'm slowly dying. Just let me sink.

Denial sets in so there is no reason to grieve. You'll be home from work soon; I'm here awaiting your return. They say as the days go by and time goes on that I will soon heal. If I'm being honest, I don't even know if I want to. If I hold on to this pain, I'll hold on to you too, right? Will I go off the deep end once reality sets in? Will healing take away the guilt I feel? Will moving on with life weaken the memories we have? I wonder... Will I ever come back from this? Will I ever be the same? What's happening to me? Why can't I feel my baby girl as I once did? Tell me, what do I do and who do I talk to? I'm frozen on the ground still calling out to you.

It's cold here...

From a Grieving Granddaughter to a Loving Grandmother

You watched me grow from a baby to a well-mannered young lady. I hope and pray that one day I will be able to meet you again. I cherished every moment until your last day because every single one was filled with joy, laughter, happiness, and unforgettable memories. Some days we laughed and some days we cried together, but there is nothing I would take back, except not having you. The talks we shared meant everything to me. You were such a wise woman that everyone respected and had great intentions toward everyone. There was not a bad bone in your body. Now that you're gone it feels weird, because we did so much together, and I miss it. We celebrated the big and small things together. I miss staying up until 12 a.m. to celebrate our birthdays together.

Words cannot express how much I miss you; it still feels unreal to me. It feels like I'm waiting on you to come home from work bumping Boosie on max volume. Without a doubt, I can say that you played a major role in my life, and I will never forget you. I love you Nana, wholeheartedly, I do. I hope you remember me up there and continue to watch over me as I continue my journey. I miss you!

Your oldest Grandbaby,
Tommy

Acknowledgments

God, I thank You for Your mercy and grace, knowing our story long before we even existed. What began as a simple prayer and a therapy session has become my greatest testimony. Thank You for turning my silence into words, my pain into purpose, and my struggles into strength. Thank You for guiding me, granting wisdom, sustaining me with Your presence, and giving me the perseverance to see this book through to completion. I am grateful for Your faithfulness, perfect timing, peace, and promises that never fail.

In loving memory of my beloved mother. Your love still surrounds me, your voice still uplifts and encourages me, and your spirit lives within me. Thank you for shaping me into the strong woman I am today, and for loving and caring for me more than I could have ever imagined. Though you are deeply missed, I carry you in my heart every day, and I couldn't ask for a greater Guardian Angel

I would like to take this time to acknowledge, in no particular order, the many people that have helped make this book and my vision possible, as well as everyone that has been part of this journey in our lives. The Williams Family is so grateful for all of you that have shown your love and care through the most unforeseen time. Although not everyone may be acknowledged here, we thank you, we love you, and we see you.

To my loud, country, but loving father, Bug, I love you. Thank you for showing us what a man is and how he should treat a woman. Mama was lucky to have you in her life. Thank you for loving her unconditionally and without restrictions. Loving her the way you did was one of the best things you could have given not only her but your children and grandchildren too. We thank you for picking up the pieces even in your pain and grief, your hurt and your sorrow. Thank you for being my safe space.

To Sterlyng, thank you for being our protector. Mama, Kaisha, and I (your girls), are so very proud of you. I have looked up to you since I was a little girl, and I am so glad to be your little sister. Thank you for doing all you can to make sure we are safe and feel loved and heard. You are our guy, and we love you. The way you stepped in and took over will never be unnoticed. You have made sure to keep Mama alive through even the smallest things, like keeping where she last rested her head still ours. Thank you for all the laughter you have brought out of us as we grieve together. Thank you for being my one call, that's all.

To my loving sister, Kaisha, you have been such an amazing sister to me and a blessing to my children and me in more ways than you will ever know. Even when we are not on the same page, you are still my girl. I cannot thank you enough. It is such a blessing to have you. You never know why God places people in your life, or you in theirs, until your time of need and despair. I understand now through you. He knew I needed you. You were meant just for our family to keep us afloat. You are our saving grace.

To my beloved children, Tommy and Papa, thank you for saving me. The two of you are my strength, my being, my world, my home. I am so grateful to have you in my life as my own. Tommy you are my favorite girl, and I hope you always know how much of me I see in you. I am in awe of your greatness and the strength you have shown thus far as the beautiful, smart young lady you are. Your strength is power, your growth is power. Your being is power. You are powerful.

To Sasha, who is my right hand, you are an amazing person. Thank you for being a sister and a safe space for me no matter the time or day. You've never judged me, even at my lowest. You picked me up off the floor and held my head up when I didn't see the road ahead to come. I appreciate your loyalty to me. Thank you for knowing me the way that no one else does.

To my dear sweet and loving Aunt P. Thank you for praying and going to war in prayer for us as you do. Thank you for allowing me to scream, shout, and cry in your arms until I couldn't anymore. Your powerful words, prayers, and wisdom to us have never failed, and as always, we love you.

Thank you to Balltop, other police officers, and the EMTs that did all they could to help our family, especially on November 10, 2022. Your service is greatly appreciated.

To PruittHealth of Swainsboro, GA, we thank you for caring for our beloved mother for twenty-three years. She not only loved her job and residents but the people she worked with as well. You are family. We thank you for giving her a safe space in the walls of your nursing home.

To Terrilski Davis, thank you for your consistent support of my book. Your mentorship and leadership have followed me throughout my military career since 2013, and still today. Thank you for encouraging me to take my journaling, even while healing, a step further by writing this book. You are appreciated.

To my previous unit, coworkers, and family of 287th QM FFC, I thank you all for your love, support, and patience you showed.

To Uncle Timmy, thank you for being the glue for us in this

time. You have shown up since the beginning, and we appreciate you more than you know. Thank you for keeping your promise to Mama.

To all our family and friends that are not listed, we thank you for your love and support through the years and more to come. We may not communicate every day or have responded to each of you individually, but we receive you and your love. Thank you for the encouraging cards, letters, and flowers. We love you and we are so proud to call you our family and friends.

To Monique Mensah, thank you for assisting me with my book, believing in me, and seeing my light. The work you do is amazing and, had it not been for you, I would still be procrastinating. You have made this process so smooth and took on most of my worries and stress. I thank you and I am so grateful for you. Thank you for your patience with me.

To Sabrina Estudillo Butler (Unpolished Words), my editor, thank you for also believing in me, our story, and my writing. Thank you for encouraging me to keep going when I felt frustrated. Your words, knowledge, and wisdom shall never go unnoticed, for your work is remarkable.

A Special Thanks

To Chapman Funeral Home of Swainsboro, GA

My family and I would like to express our gratitude for all you have done. We received above and beyond traditional care. We appreciate your help, time, patience, and professionalism in the most vulnerable time of our lives. Many would say that you were simply doing your job, but to us, your support helped show a way forward during this challenging transition, and for that, we are so humbly grateful for you and the extended care you have graced upon our family. Thank you for caring for Johnnie "Etta," our mother, as much as we did in her transition. We appreciate each of you. May God continue to bless you all, your families, your business, and beyond.

Thank You,
The Williams Family

Discussion Questions

1. What moment in this story touched you the most, and why?
2. What part/parts of the story did you like most?
3. How has pain or loss shaped the way you see yourself today?
4. What does healing look like for you right now?
5. Have you ever felt silenced by your own experiences? What helped you find your voice again?
6. How do you define love after experiencing hurt or loss?
7. How can we honor the memories of those we've lost while continuing to live fully?
8. When life feels unbearable, what keeps you going?
9. How has faith in yourself, God, or life helped you survive hard seasons?
10. What does strength look like when you don't feel strong?
11. What does it mean to "turn pain into purpose" in your own life?
12. What signs of unhealthy or abusive behavior do you think people often overlook?
13. What signs of abusive behaviors in this story did you notice?

14. Why do you think it's hard for survivors to speak up and what can make it easier?
15. How can friends, family, or communities better support survivors?
16. What message would you share with someone currently living in fear or silence?
17. What truth have you discovered about yourself through pain?

Resources

Domestic Violence Support

National Domestic Violence Hotline (USA) Call or Text: 1-800-799-SAFE (7233) Website: www.thehotline.org. Confidential support, safety planning, and resources for survivors.

RAINN (Rape, Abuse & Incest National Network) Call: 1-800-656-4673 Website: www.rainn.org. Support for sexual assault survivors and confidential counseling.

Love Is Respect Call or Text: 1-866-331-9474 Website: www.loveisrespect.org. Support for young adults experiencing dating abuse.

Mental Health Support

National Alliance on Mental Illness (NAMI) Helpline: 1-800-950-6264 Website: www.nami.org. Offers education, support groups, and guidance for mental health conditions.

Mental Health America (MHA) Website: www.mhanational.org. Provides mental health screenings, resources, and advocacy.

988 Suicide & Crisis Lifeline (USA) Dial: 988 Text: "HELLO" to 741741 Website: www.988lifeline.org. 24/7 confidential support for emotional crises or suicidal thoughts.

Therapy and Counseling

Psychology Today – Find a Therapist Website: www.psychologytoday.com/us/therapists. Search for licensed therapists and counselors near you or for online therapy.

BetterHelp Website: www.betterhelp.com. Online therapy with licensed counselors.

Open Path Collective Website: www.openpathcollective.org. Affordable in-person and online therapy options.

Additional Support & Information

Childhelp. Child abuse prevention and support. Call: 1-800-422-4453 Website: www.childhelp.org

SAMHSA (Substance Abuse & Mental Health Services Administration) Helpline: 1-800-662-4357 Website: www.samhsa.gov. Support for substance abuse and mental health treatment resources.

Local Community Resources. Many cities and counties have local domestic violence shelters, mental health clinics, and support groups. You can search online or call your local health department for information.

Spotify Playlist

Music has been one of my lifelines in the years since losing my mother, Etta, especially in the moments when grief blurred my sense of self.

I've gathered the songs that carried me through. Scan the QR code below to access **Etta's Song playlist** on Spotify.